Diet recommendations during colon cancer

Diet can support the affected organs and is not a treatment for the disease. Please check these recommendations always with a nutrition consultant, therapist, doctor or dietician. The recipes and the list of ingredients are supporting the conventional medical therapy. The calorie disclosures of fresh ingredients (fruit and vegetables) vary according to quality and time of harvest. The contents were checked by a dietician and a nutrition consultant for the Traditional Chinese Medicine (TCM).

Author:
©2017 Josef Miligui
www.ebns.at

AF199856

Source:
The lists are created from the EBNS database for nutritional counseling. The database is used by dietitians, therapists and doctors for advising the patient / client.

Literature:
The specialist literature and the training documents of the German and Austrian dietary and traditional Chinese medicine serve as a knowledge base. We have used the documents as a basis of knowledge, adapted it to our experience and completed them.
http://di-book.com

Title Photo:
©2008 Erika Weixlbaumer

Production and publishing:
BoD – Books on Demand, Norderstedt
ISBN: 9783746098098

Diet recommendations during colon cancer

1   Treatment strategy...5
2   Avoid 5
3   Breakfast kkal. per serving...5
4   Snack 6
5   Lunch 6
6   Afternoon...8
7   Dinner...8
8   Any time 10
9   Recipes 11
   9.1   Antipasti..11
   9.2   Apple - banana cream..12
   9.3   Apricot Oat Balls with Acai powder.........................12
   9.4   Avocado with lemon..13
   9.5   Barley and vegetable soup.......................................13
   9.6   Barley mash with steamed pear 14
   9.7   Basic recipe for a chicken broth worming...............15
   9.8   Basic recipe for a fish broth.....................................15
   9.9   Basic recipe for a vegetable soup, nutritious.........16
   9.10   Beluga lentil stew with vegetables...........................17
   9.11   Bilberry - curd cheese with Acai powder.................18
   9.12   Blueberry puree 19
   9.13   Boiled celery salad with exotic spices.....................19
   9.14   Broccoli cream soup 20
   9.15   Bulgur with tomatoes and fresh herbs 21
   9.16   Cardamom water...21
   9.17   Carrot and potato rucola sandwich..........................22
   9.18   Carrot and rice gruel soup..23
   9.19   Carrot Risotto 23
   9.20   Celery and potato cream soup 24
   9.21   Celery juice..25
   9.22   Celery salad with lemon and olive oil.......................25
   9.23   Chicken in an ilalian style...25
   9.24   Chicken soup with egg yolk and parsley..................27
   9.25   Chicken soup with green spelt, parsley and sake ...27
   9.26   Chicken with white turnips on rice 28
   9.27   Coconut rice with cardamom.....................................29
   9.28   Compote from blueberries...30
   9.29   Compote of pears 30
   9.30   Cottage cheese with steamed fruit 31

9.31	Couscous Salad	31
9.32	Cranberry juice	32
9.33	Cucumber soup	32
9.34	Duck soup with algae	33
9.35	Fennel and potato gratin	34
9.36	Figs with mozzarella and honey	35
9.37	Fish soup with rosemary	36
9.38	Fried asparagus with rocket	36
9.39	Grated apple	37
9.40	Grilled salmon steaks with cauliflower and potatoes	37
9.41	Grilled tofu with rice noodles, spinach and sugar snaps	39
9.42	Halibut with tomato and garlic sauce	40
9.43	Japanese algae soup	41
9.44	Mango banana yoghurt drink ice cold	41
9.45	Marinated cod on pumpkin puree	42
9.46	Marinated courgette with smoked tofu	43
9.47	Melanzani with olive oil and turmeric	44
9.48	Milk rice vanilla - with cherries	44
9.49	Noodles with turkeymeat and pineapple	45
9.50	Noodles with vegetable and tomato sauce	46
9.51	Oatmeal soup with spring onion and carrots	47
9.52	Oven potatoes with celery-curd cheese (quark)	47
9.53	Pancakes with spinach and parmesan	48
9.54	Pear compote	49
9.55	Polenta with fried egg	50
9.56	Potato cream with herbs and fresh cheese	50
9.57	Potato gnocchi with vegetables and basil sauce	51
9.58	Potato-basil soup	52
9.59	Potatoes with curd cheese sauce	53
9.60	Pumpkin curry	54
9.61	Pumpkin dumplings with tomato and parsley sauce	55
9.62	Quinoa piquant with avocado	56
9.63	Quinoa with peach	57
9.64	Radish with horseradish	57
9.65	Refreshing cucumber soup with potatoes	58
9.66	Rice congee with honey pear and black sesame	59
9.67	Rice noodle soup with shiitake mushrooms	59
9.68	Rice with parsnips	60
9.69	Rice with stewed vegetables	61
9.70	Roasted barley patties	61
9.71	Rosemary Potatoes	62
9.72	Salmon on tomato-spinach	63
9.73	Semolina dumpling & mascarpone and strawberry sauce	64

9.74	Semolina porridge with banana	65
9.75	Sliced chicken with walnuts and sherry	65
9.76	Sliced turkey with zucchini	66
9.77	Spelled-grid porridge with berries of the season	67
9.78	Strawberry bananas mash	68
9.79	Supplementary nutrition	68
9.80	Sweet potato pancakes with basil pesto	69
9.81	Tea from anise	70
9.82	Tea from fennel	70
9.83	Tea from ginger with honey	71
9.84	Tea from yarrow	71
9.85	Tea Green tea	72
9.86	Tea mixture against intestinal inertia	72
9.87	Tea mixture appetizing	73
9.88	Tomato soup	73
9.89	Tomato with mozzarella	74
9.90	Vegetable bowl with Provencal pistou	75
9.91	Vitamin drink	76
9.92	Warming carrot soup	76
9.93	Wheat fresh grain porridge with pears.	77
9.94	Yellow lentil soup	78
10	Effects of food	79
10.1	Use ingredients: recommendable	79
10.2	Use ingredients: yes	80
10.3	Use ingredients: little	85
10.4	Do not use contra-acting foods	86
11	Herbs and their effects	86
11.1	Basil	86
11.2	Nettles	87
11.3	Dill	87
11.4	Coriander	87
11.5	Herbs various	87
11.6	Cress	87
11.7	Chives	87
11.8	Lovage	87
11.9	Dandelion (young plants)	87
11.10	Oregano fresh	88
11.11	Oregano dried	88
11.12	Parsley	88
11.13	Peppermint	88
11.14	Rosemary	88
11.15	Sage	88
11.16	Blackthorn (Sloe)	88

11.17	Black caraway	89
11.18	Thyme dried	89
11.19	Lemongrass	89
11.20	Lemon Balm	89
12 Basics of Nutrition		90
12.1	Nutrition	90
12.2	Recipes	92
12.3	Foodstuffs	92
12.4	Herbs	93
13 Other dietic-books		94

1 Treatment strategy

Sufficient fiber intake, sufficient intake of drinking fluid, preferably water. Vegetables and whole grains should be eaten in larger quantities and become the main component of the diet. Fish and poultry should be preferred over red meat. The alcohol consumption should not exceed the amount of 20 g / day.

2 Avoid

High fat, low-fiber foods, high meat consumption, high calcium intake (hard cheese, parmesan, Emmentaler, Gauda, Edam, Gorgonzola, ...) Soya products in large quantities, red meat.

3 Breakfast   kkal. per serving

Apple - banana cream	110
Avocado with lemon	289
Barley and vegetable soup	281
Blueberry puree	10
Bulgur with tomatoes and fresh herbs	205
Carrot and potato rucola sandwich	94
Carrot and rice gruel soup	101
Celery juice	33
Coconut rice with cardamom	266
Compote from blueberries	49
Cottage cheese with steamed fruit	214
Couscous Salad	338
Cranberry juice	43
Grated apple	120

Noodles with vegetable and tomato sauce................................. 561
Oatmeal soup with spring onion and carrots 134
Polenta with fried egg.. 410
Potato cream with herbs and fresh cheese 217
Potato-basil soup 95
Quinoa piquant with avocado 561
Quinoa with peach 247
Radish with horseradish... 196
Refreshing cucumber soup with potatoes............................... 148
Rice congee with honey pear and black sesame 158
Rice noodle soup with shiitake mushrooms 65
Rice with parsnips... 206
Roasted barley patties 398
Rosemary Potatoes.. 188
Semolina dumpling with mascarpone and strawberry sauce 331
Semolina porridge with banana 307
Spelled-grid porridge with berries of the season 243
Supplementary nutrition 1045
Tea from anise... 2
Tea from fennel.. 0
Tea from ginger with honey.. 4
Tea Green tea... 2
Vitamin drink... 172
Wheat fresh grain porridge with pears. 309

4 Snack

Apple - banana cream... 110
Carrot and potato rucola sandwich...................................... 94
Figs with mozzarella and honey 415
Spelled-grid porridge with berries of the season 243

5 Lunch

Antipasti.. 100
Avocado with lemon... 289
Barley and vegetable soup.. 281
Barley mash with steamed pear 113
Beluga lentil stew with vegetables 201
Blueberry puree 10
Boiled celery salad with exotic spices................................... 165
Broccoli cream soup... 98
Bulgur with tomatoes and fresh herbs.................................... 205
Carrot and potato rucola sandwich 94

Carrot and rice gruel soup 101
Carrot Risotto.. 308
Celery and potato cream soup... 112
Celery juice 33
Chicken in an ilalian style 410
Chicken soup with egg yolk and parsley 117
Chicken soup with green spelt, parsley and sake.......................... 150
Chicken with white turnips on rice.. 323
Coconut rice with cardamom 266
Compote from blueberries... 49
Compote of pears 122
Cottage cheese with steamed fruit.. 214
Couscous Salad.. 338
Cranberry juice... 43
Cucumber soup... 95
Duck soup with algae 664
Fennel and potato gratin 147
Fish soup with rosemary 271
Fried asparagus with rocket 148
Grated apple 120
Grilled salmon steaks with cauliflower and potatoes 329
Grilled tofu with rice noodles, spinach and sugar snaps 327
Halibut with tomato and garlic sauce 319
Japanese algae soup 47
Mango banana yoghurt drink ice cold 121
Marinated cod on pumpkin puree 201
Marinated courgette with smoked tofu 132
Melanzani with olive oil and turmeric 432
Noodles with turkeymeat and pineapple 291
Noodles with vegetable and tomato sauce.................................... 561
Oatmeal soup with spring onion and carrots 134
Oven potatoes with celery-curd cheese (quark)............................ 304
Pancakes with spinach and parmesan.. 329
Pear compote 100
Polenta with fried egg.. 410
Potato cream with herbs and fresh cheese 217
Potato gnocchi with vegetables and basil sauce 166
Potato-basil soup 95
Potatoes with curd cheese sauce 413
Pumpkin curry.. 193
Pumpkin dumplings with tomato and parsley sauce....................... 380
Radish with horseradish 196
Refreshing cucumber soup with potatoes 148

Rice congee with honey pear and black sesame 158
Rice noodle soup with shiitake mushrooms 65
Rice with parsnips 206
Rice with stewed vegetables 166
Roasted barley patties 398
Rosemary Potatoes 188
Salmon on tomato-spinach 364
Semolina dumpling with mascarpone and strawberry sauce 331
Semolina porridge with banana 307
Sliced chicken with walnuts and sherry 304
Sliced turkey with zucchini - Also for babies from the 12th month .. 281
Spelled-grid porridge with berries of the season 243
Supplementary nutrition 1045
Sweet potato pancakes with basil pesto 625
Tea from anise 2
Tea from fennel 0
Tea from ginger with honey 4
Tea Green tea 2
Tomato soup 100
Tomato with mozzarella 436
Vegetable bowl with Provencal pistou 137
Vitamin drink 172
Warming carrot soup 133
Wheat fresh grain porridge with pears. 309
Yellow lentil soup 155

6 Afternoon

Apple - banana cream 110
Carrot and potato rucola sandwich 94
Figs with mozzarella and honey 415
Spelled-grid porridge with berries of the season 243

7 Dinner

Avocado with lemon 289
Barley and vegetable soup 281
Beluga lentil stew with vegetables 201
Blueberry puree 10
Boiled celery salad with exotic spices 165
Broccoli cream soup 98
Carrot Risotto 308
Celery and potato cream soup 112
Celery juice 33

Chicken in an ilalian style 410
Chicken with white turnips on rice.. 323
Coconut rice with cardamom 266
Compote from blueberries.. 49
Compote of pears 122
Cranberry juice.. 43
Duck soup with algae 664
Fennel and potato gratin 147
Fish soup with rosemary 271
Fried asparagus with rocket 148
Grated apple.. 120
Grilled salmon steaks with cauliflower and potatoes 329
Grilled tofu with rice noodles, spinach and sugar snaps.............. 327
Halibut with tomato and garlic sauce 319
Japanese algae soup 47
Mango banana yoghurt drink ice cold 121
Marinated cod on pumpkin puree 201
Marinated courgette with smoked tofu.. 132
Melanzani with olive oil and turmeric 432
Noodles with turkeymeat and pineapple 291
Noodles with vegetable and tomato sauce.................................. 561
Oven potatoes with celery-curd cheese (quark)........................... 304
Pancakes with spinach and parmesan... 329
Pear compote 100
Polenta with fried egg.. 410
Potato gnocchi with vegetables and basil sauce 166
Potato-basil soup 95
Potatoes with curd cheese sauce 413
Pumpkin curry.. 193
Pumpkin dumplings with tomato and parsley sauce..................... 380
Quinoa piquant with avocado 561
Quinoa with peach 247
Radish with horseradish 196
Refreshing cucumber soup with potatoes 148
Rice congee with honey pear and black sesame 158
Rice noodle soup with shiitake mushrooms 65
Rice with parsnips.. 206
Rice with stewed vegetables 166
Roasted barley patties 398
Rosemary Potatoes.. 188
Salmon on tomato-spinach... 364
Semolina porridge with banana 307
Sliced chicken with walnuts and sherry....................................... 304

Sliced turkey with zucchini...... 281
Spelled-grid porridge with berries of the season 243
Supplementary nutrition 1045
Sweet potato pancakes with basil pesto 625
Tea from anise...... 2
Tea from fennel...... 0
Tea from ginger with honey...... 4
Tea Green tea...... 2
Tomato soup...... 100
Tomato with mozzarella 436
Vegetable bowl with Provencal pistou...... 137
Vitamin drink...... 172
Warming carrot soup...... 133
Wheat fresh grain porridge with pears. 309
Yellow lentil soup 155

8 Any time

Apricot Oat Balls with Acai powder...... 768
Avocado with lemon...... 289
Bilberry - curd cheese with Acai powder 237
Blueberry puree 10
Carrot and rice gruel soup...... 101
Celery juice...... 33
Coconut rice with cardamom...... 266
Compote from blueberries...... 49
Compote of pears 122
Cranberry juice...... 43
Grated apple...... 120
Mango banana yoghurt drink ice cold 121
Milk rice vanilla - with cherries...... 394
Pear compote 100
Rice congee with honey pear and black sesame 158
Rice with parsnips...... 206
Semolina porridge with banana 307
Strawberry bananas mash...... 30
Supplementary nutrition 1045
Tea from anise...... 2
Tea from fennel...... 0
Tea from ginger with honey...... 4
Tea Green tea...... 2
Wheat fresh grain porridge with pears. 309

9 Recipes

(recommendable) = You can use more.
(little) = You should use less than specified or omit.

9.1 Antipasti

Improves blood circulation, anti-inflammatory, relieves pain. Diuretic, promotes digestion, reduces blood pressure. antioxidativ, antibacterial, affects anorexia, improves digestion, flatulence, stomach weakness, stimulating.
Cooking time approx. 40 min
Calories p. portion: 100
3 portions
Allergens:

Quantity of ingredients:
Pepperoni 1 piece / 5g. (little)
Lemon juice 1 table spoon / 10g. (yes)
Aubergine 1 piece / 300g. (recommended)
Tomato 4 pieces / 200g. (recommended)
Zucchini 5/8 oz / 200g. (recommended)
Lemon peel 1/2 piece / 3g. (yes)
Olive oil 1 table spoon / 15g. (yes)
Basil (fresh) 8 leaves / 5g. (recommended)
Salt 1 pinch / 0,5g. (little)
Coriander 1/2 teaspoon / 2g. (recommended)

Cooking instructions:
Preheat the oven to 250 degrees Celsius and bake the hot peppers until the bowl becomes dark (about 20 minutes). Cover the hot peppers with a clear film and allow to cool. Peel the skin and cut into strips about 2 cm wide. Cut tomatoes in half and spread with oil in slices of aubergine and bake in the oven at 200 degrees golden brown (about 10 minutes) Fry the zucchini slices in the grill pan (without fat).
Mix everything together, mix the marinade of olive oil, salt and lemon peel and pour over the vegetables, sprinkle with coriander. Leave for 1 hour.

9.2 Apple - banana cream

Regulates gastrointestinal function, provides vitamin C, cholesterol lowering, reduces inflammation, diuretic, improves blood circulation.
Cooking time approx. 15 min
Calories p. portion: 110
4 portions
Allergens:

Quantity of ingredients:
Apple (sour) 7/8 lbs / 400g. (recommended)
Water 3/4 cup - 6 oz / 200g. (yes)
Orange peel 1/4 piece / 5g. (yes)
Lemon peel 1/2 piece / 2g. (yes)
Sugar brown 2 teaspoons / 6g. (little)
Cinnamon sticks 1 piece / 0g. (recommended)
Banana 1 piece / 150g. (recommended)
Acerola fruit nectar or powder 1 teaspoon / 2g. (recommended)
Orange juice 1/2 piece / 50g. (recommended)
Lemon juice 1 table spoon / 10g. (yes)

Cooking instructions:
Cut the apple into fine slices, bring water to boil and add the apple slices, orange- and lemon peel, sugar and cinnamon and simmer about 7 minutes. The apples should be almost soft. Remove acerola and the cinnamon stick. Mix the apple, the banana, the orange juice and the lemon juice.

9.3 Apricot Oat Balls with Acai powder

Strengthens immune system, little laxative, antioxidativ.
Cooking time approx. 20 min
Calories p. portion: 768
2 portions
Allergens: AHO

Quantity of ingredients:
Oat flakes (whole grain) 1/4 lbs - 4oz / 125g. (yes)
Apricot dried 1/4 lbs - 4oz / 125g. (yes)
Almond 1/4 lbs - 4oz / 100g. (yes)
Honey 2 table spoons / 14g. (yes)
Acai powder 3 teaspoons / 9g. (recommended)
Lemon juice 2 table spoons / 9g. (yes)

Cooking instructions:
Lightly chop the sliced almonds in the pan and let them cool. Then pour the apricots in the blender and add lemon juice. Mix all the ingredients together. If the mass is too loose add some honey. Finally, form small balls and roll them in oat flakes.

9.4 Avocado with lemon

Good to fight insomnia, inflammation, swelling, pain and itching. Is calming.
Cooking time approx. 5 min
Calories p. portion: 289
1 portions
Allergens:

Quantity of ingredients:
Avocado 1/2 piece / 120g. (recommended)
Lemon juice 1/2 piece / 10g. (yes)
Salt 1 pinch / 1g. (little)

Cooking instructions:
Halve the avocado, remove the core, add the lemon juice, salt a little and eat with a spoon.

9.5 Barley and vegetable soup

Supports urination, detoxifying, promotes spleen and liver, reduces blood pressure, strengthens immune system, prevents cancer, reduces radiation damage, promotes digestion, helps to digest fat, harmonizes metabolism.
Cooking time approx. 2 hours
Calories p. portion: 281
3 portions
Allergens: AGL

Quantity of ingredients:
Barley 1 cup / 120g. (yes)
Shiitake, dried 1/8 oz / 4g. (yes)
Onion (shallot) 1 piece / 20g. (little)
Cumin (Caraway seed) 1 knife tip / 0,5g. (recommended)
Sunflower oil 1 table spoon / 10g. (yes)
Water 1 cup / 250g. (yes)
Celery sticks 2 branches / 20g. (recommended)
Peas, green 5/8 lbs - 8oz / 250g. (recommended)

Tomato 1 piece / 50g. (recommended)
Carrot 2 pieces / 150g. (recommended)
French beans Handful / 30g. (little)
Salt 1 pinch / 1g. (little)
Pepper (ground) 1 pinch / 0,5g. (little)
Parsley 1 teaspoon / 3g. (recommended)
Butter organic 1 teaspoon / 3g. (yes)

Cooking instructions:
Soak the barley in the evening for the next day. Soak the mushrooms separately at the next day. Brown onion and cumin in oil, then boil with water. Add the chopped vegetables, some salt, the barley and the shiitake mushrooms and cook everything to a thick soup. At the end, season with pepper, parsley and a little butter.

9.6 Barley mash with steamed pear

Promotes digestion, supports urination, promotes spleen, diuretic, forcing spleen, relaxes, promotes perspiration.
Cooking time approx. 25 min
Calories p. portion: 114
5 portions
Allergens: A

Quantity of ingredients:
Water 10 cups / 1200g. (yes)
Barley 1 cup / 120g. (yes)
Ginger fresh 2 slices / 2g. (recommended)
Cardamom 3 capsules / 1g. (recommended)
Salt 1 pinch / 1g. (little)
Pear 1 piece / 200g. (recommended)
Sugar cane sugar 1/2 teaspoon / 5g. (little)

Cooking instructions:
Grind coarse the barley and roast it dry. Add hot water, add ginger and cardamom and let it swell to a pulp in low heat. Peel and dice the pear and boil for 10 minutes with a little water. At the end, add the stewed pear, a little butter and sweetener.

Variant: If you want to go fast, you can use barley flakes instead of shot.

9.7 Basic recipe for a chicken broth worming

Strengthens blood, strengthens bone marrow, reduces blood pressure, strengthens immune system, prevents cancer, reduces radiation damage, promotes sweating, dissolves stagnation, good to fight loss of appetite, flatulence.
Cooking time approx. 2-3 hours
Calories p. portion: 90
9 portions
Allergens: L

Quantity of ingredients:
Chicken meat 1/2 piece / 600g. (yes)
Carrot 2 pieces / 150g. (recommended)
Leek 1 stick / 45g. (little)
Celery root 1 piece / 500g. (recommended)
Ginger fresh 2 slices / 2g. (recommended)
Fenugreek (Trigonella foenum-graecum) 1 teaspoon / 2g. (yes)
Juniper berry 1 teaspoon / 3g. (yes)
Bay leaf 3 pieces / 2g. (recommended)
Water 4 cup / 900g. (yes)

Cooking instructions:
Remove chicken parts from fat. Place chicken pieces in a saucepan with hot water and heat till it boils briefly, skimming any resulting foam. Add coarsely chopped vegetables and all spices and cook over medium heat for 2 to 3 hours. Strain the finished soup. Throw away vegetables and bones.
Tip: If you want to use the meat as a soup insert, take out after 45 minutes and return only the bones in the soup.
Refrigerate for later use.

9.8 Basic recipe for a fish broth

Strengthens the kidneys, promotes watering, reduces blood pressure, strengthens immune system, prevents cancer, reduces radiation damage. Low in cholesterol and protein rich. Improves blood circulation, stimulates appetite.
Cooking time approx. 40 min
Calories p. portion: 128
5 portions
Allergens: DLO

Quantity of ingredients:
Fish pieces mixed (fresh water) 3/4 lbs / 300g. (recommended)
Celery root 1/4 lbs - 4oz / 120g. (recommended)
Leek 2 inches / 10g. (little)
Carrot 2 pieces / 150g. (recommended)
White wine 1/2 cup / 125g. (little)
Lemon 1/2 piece / 50g. (yes)
Bay leaf 2 leaves / 2g. (recommended)
Peppercorns 3 pieces / 2g. (little)
Olive oil 1 table spoon / 10g. (yes)
Water 2 cup / 450g. (yes)

Cooking instructions:
Fry celery, chopped carrots and leeks in olive oil, add bay leaf and peppercorns, add pieces of fish and sauté briefly. Add water, add little white wine or lemon. Simmer gently for 30 minutes. Skim off the resulting foam several times. In the end, sift the ingredients through a cloth.
Refrigerate for later use

9.9   Basic recipe for a vegetable soup, nutritious

Reduces blood pressure, strengthens immune system, prevents cancer, forcing spleen, dissolves stagnation, promotes weight loss. Good to fight immunodeficiency, high blood pressure, depressions, diabetes, diarrhea, reduces blood lipids.
Cooking time approx. 2-3 hours
Calories p. portion: 48
5 portions
Allergens: L

Quantity of ingredients:
Olive oil 1 table spoon / 4g. (yes)
Onion white 1 piece / 60g. (little)
Carrot 3 pieces / 200g. (recommended)
Parsnip 3/8 lbs - 6oz / 150g. (recommended)
Celery root 1 cup / 100g. (recommended)
Ginger fresh 1/2 teaspoon / 2g. (recommended)
Lemon 1/2 piece / 25g. (yes)
Juniper berry 6 pieces / 6g. (yes)
Thyme dried 1 pinch / 1g. (yes)
Lovage 1 table spoon / 3g. (recommended)
Bay leaf 2 leaves / 1g. (recommended)

Salt 1 pinch / 1g. (little)
Water 3 cups / 650g. (yes)

Cooking instructions:
Cut the vegetables into cubes.
Heat oil in hot pot, fry shortly onions and vegetables.
Add cold water, then add ginger, bay leaf and lemon juice.
Season with juniper, thyme and lovage. Cover for 2 - 3 hours on a low heat and simmer.
The used vegetables should be thrown away.
The basic recipe serves as a soup base and to refine vegetables, legumes or cereals.
If you want to eat vegetable soup immediately, add the desired vegetables half an hour before.
Refrigerate for later use.

9.10 Beluga lentil stew with vegetables

Promotes sweating, dissolves stagnation. Relieves constipation, strengthens mother milk production, stimulates nerves, detoxifying, reduces inflammation, improves blood circulation. Strengthens heart and kidney, diuretic, calms the stomach, promotes digestion.
Cooking time approx. 20 min
Calories p. portion: 201
5 portions
Allergens:

Quantity of ingredients:
Lentils 1 1/2 cups / 240g. (little)
Water 4-5 cups / 500g. (yes)
Carrot 3 pieces / 150g. (recommended)
Leek 1 piece / 300g. (little)
Kohlrabi 1/2 piece / 200g. (recommended)
Tomato 2 pieces / 80g. (recommended)
Onion white 1 piece / 50g. (little)
Bay leaf 2 leaves / 1g. (recommended)
Fennel 1 piece / 250g. (recommended)
Star anise 2 pieces / 1g. (yes)
Juniper berry 6 pieces / 2g. (yes)
Olive oil 2 table spoons / 30g. (yes)
Salt 1 pinch / 1g. (little)
Ginger fresh 1/2 teaspoon / 2g. (recommended)
Black caraway 1 pinch / 1g. (yes)

Cooking instructions:
Heat oil in hot pot. Fry onions and add diced vegetables and spices, lentils (washed well) and salt. Cover with cold water (3 fingers wide) and cook for 20 minutes on a low heat.
Sprinkle with fresh herbs and black cumin

Goes well with rice!

9.11 Bilberry - curd cheese with Acai powder

Good to fight weakness, belching, diabetes, acute or chronic obstruction of the bowel, skin problems. Laxative, antibacterial effect. Antioxidant.
Cooking time approx. 10 min
Calories p. portion: 238
2 portions
Allergens: GH

Quantity of ingredients:
Blueberry 5/8 oz / 200g. (yes)
Orange juice 2 table spoons / 10g. (recommended)
Maple syrup 1 table spoon / 5g. (recommended)
Almond 1 table spoon / 5g. (yes)
Curd cheese 20% 5/8 lbs - 8oz / 250g. (yes)
Sugar cane sugar 1 table spoon / 9g. (little)
Acai powder 2 teaspoons / 5g. (recommended)
Cinnamon ground 1 pinch / 0,5g. (recommended)

Cooking instructions:
Rinse the blueberries in a sieve and pat dry gently. Drizzle with orange juice and maple syrup and stir in the Acai powder.

Roast the almond sticks in a frying pan until golden brown until they are fragrant and allow to cool on a plate. Dust with a little cinnamon.

Stir quark and sugar until smooth.

Layer alternately the quark with the marinated blueberries in glasses and garnish with the almonds.

9.12 Blueberry puree

Bilberry is laxative. Clove dissolves stagnation. Cinnamon powder heats stomach and spleen, improves blood circulation.
Cooking time approx. 10 min
Calories p. portion: 10
1 portions
Allergens:

Quantity of ingredients:
Blueberry 1/2 oz / 20g. (yes)
Cinnamon ground 1 pinch / 0,1g. (recommended)
Clove 1 piece / 1g. (yes)
Water 1 cup / 250g. (yes)

Cooking instructions:
Boil blueberries with cinnamon and clove in water for 10 minutes. Remove the cinnamon and clove. Puree. Sweet as desired.

9.13 Boiled celery salad with exotic spices

Forcing spleen, relieves diarrhea, antibacterial, blood-forming, blood detoxifying, reduces inflammation, diuretic, improves blood circulation.
Cooking time approx. 30 min
Calories p. portion: 166
4 portions
Allergens: GLMNO

Quantity of ingredients:
Celery root 1 1/2 piece / 900g. (recommended)
Yogurt (natural, 3.5% fat) 1 cup / 250g. (yes)
Sour cream 15% fat 2 table spoons / 20g. (yes)
Turmeric (yellow root) 1 pinch / 1g. (recommended)
Sesame oil 1 table spoon / 20g. (yes)
Pepper (ground) 1 pinch / 0,5g. (little)
Lemongrass 1 pinch / 1g. (yes)
Onion white 1/2 piece / 25g. (little)
Mustard 1/2 teaspoon / 1g. (yes)
Black caraway 1 pinch / 1g. (yes)
Salt 1 pinch / 1g. (little)
Lemon juice 1 piece / 40g. (yes)
Apple (sour) 1/2 piece / 100g. (recommended)
Peppers powder 1 pinch / 1g. (yes)
Vinegar (Apple vinegar) 1 dash / 3g. (yes)

Cooking instructions:
Cook the peeled celeriac in thick slices and then cut into bite-sized strips.
Dressing: Mix a little yoghurt, sour cream, turmeric, sesame oil, pepper, lemongrass powder, finely chopped onion, a little mustard, salt, crushed black cumin, some cold water, lemon juice or vinegar; add the sour chopped apple, some rose paprika, the lukewarm celery and mix well; let it rest for 2 - 3 hours or overnight.
Ideal as a substitute for raw food

9.14 Broccoli cream soup

Strengthen your immune system, build and maintain healthy bones, teeth, hair and nails. Reduces blood pressure, strengthens immune system, prevents cancer, reduces radiation damage.
Cooking time approx. 30 min
Calories p. portion: 98
6 portions
Allergens: LO

Quantity of ingredients:
Olive oil 2 table spoons / 7g. (yes)
Broccoli 1,1 lbs / 500g. (recommended)
Carrot 2 pieces / 150g. (recommended)
Potato 2 pieces / 120g. (recommended)
Onion white 1 piece / 50g. (little)
Water 1 cup / 50g. (yes)
Basic recipe for a vegetable soup 2 cup / 500g. (recommended)
White wine 1/2 cup / 125g. (little)
Sage 1 teaspoon / 2g. (yes)
Rosemary 1 teaspoon / 2g. (yes)
Pepper (ground) 1 pinch / 0,5g. (little)
Salt 1 pinch / 1g. (little)

Cooking instructions:
Add the olive oil to the pan, add the washed and cut broccoli, diced carrots and potatoes, sauté for a short time, add the chopped onion, fill with water, enough water to cover the vegetables at least 3 finger breadths. Add bouillon, salt, add a little bit of white wine, add the seasoned sage and rosemary.
Heat till it boils and then simmer on a small fire for about 25 minutes.
Season with pepper, if necessary season with sea salt. Purée the soup.

9.15 Bulgur with tomatoes and fresh herbs

Promotes digestion, helps to digest fat, supports urination, reduces blood pressure. Stimulates digestion, supports urination.
Cooking time approx. 30 min
Calories p. portion: 205
1 portions
Allergens: A

Quantity of ingredients:
Bulgur (cereals) 1 cup / 120g. (yes)
Tomato 2 pieces / 70g. (recommended)
Rucola 2 table spoons / 16g. (yes)
Pepper powder (hot) 1 pinch / 2g. (yes)
Olive oil 2 table spoons / 20g. (yes)
Pepper (ground) 1 pinch / 0,5g. (little)
Salt 1 pinch / 1g. (little)
Basil 4 leaves / 2g. (recommended)
Thyme 1 Twig / 3g. (yes)
Lemon juice 1/2 piece / 10g. (yes)

Cooking instructions:
Put cold water in a pot, sprinkle in Bulgur and simmer. Stir in chopped tomatoes, fresh herbs like basil, thyme, arugula, a pinch of rose paprika, lemon juice, a dash of olive oil, a little ground pepper, some salt.

Variant: add some mozzarella.

Recommendation: ideal morning meal in summer; also suitable as evening meal, especially for sleep disorders.

9.16 Cardamom water

Promotes digestion, nourishes bones and tendons, warms kidneys and spleen, forcing spleen, neutralizes flatulence, controls excessive urge to urinate, helps to fight digestive weakness.
Cooking time approx. 20 min
Calories p. portion: 16
4 portions
Allergens:

Quantity of ingredients:
Cardamom 2 table spoons / 18g. (recommended)
Water 4 cup / 1000g. (yes)

Cooking instructions:
Finely crush cardamom pods in a mortar. Boil with 1 liter of water and cook gently for 10 minutes over medium heat. Fill cardamom water through a sieve in glasses and serve hot.

9.17 Carrot and potato rucola sandwich

Reduces inflammation, improves digestion, supports urination, lowers cholesterol, strengthens immune system, prevents cancer, good to fight constipation (Fibre-rich), dissolves stagnation.
Cooking time approx. 20 min
Calories p. portion: 94
4 portions
Allergens: AG

Quantity of ingredients:
Potato (mealy) 5/8 oz / 200g. (recommended)
Carrot 1 piece / 50g. (recommended)
Sour cream 15% fat 2 table spoons / 45g. (yes)
Onion (spring onion) 1 piece / 20g. (little)
Rucola 1/2 bunch / 100g. (yes)
Lemon peel 1/4 teaspoon / 1g. (yes)
Salt 1 pinch / 1g. (little)
Pepper (ground) 1 pinch / 0,2g. (little)
Whole grain bread 8 slices / 48g. (recommended)

Cooking instructions:
Cook the potatoes gently, peel and squeeze through the potato press.
Cook vegetable broth according to the basic recipe and remove a carrot after a short cooking time and finely crush with a fork.
Stir the potatoes, carrots, grated lemon zest and sour cream into a smooth cream.
Mix carrot and potato cream with finely chopped rocket salad. Season the spread with salt and pepper and spread the bread. Sprinkle with the finely chopped young onions.

9.18 Carrot and rice gruel soup

Stops diarrhea, good to fight fever, strengthens immune system,
reduces blood pressure.
Cooking time approx. 10 min
Calories p. portion: 101
1 portions
Allergens:

Quantity of ingredients:
Basic recipe for a rice soup (Congee) 1 cup / 120g. (recommended)
Carrot 2 pieces / 100g. (recommended)
Salt 1 teaspoon / 4g. (little)

Cooking instructions:
Peel and grate carrots. Heat the rice soup (according to the basic
recipe) till it boils and add the grated carrots and salt. Cook for 10
minutes.

9.19 Carrot Risotto

Strengthens immune system, prevents cancer, loss of appetite,
flatulence, high blood pressure, depressions, diabetes, diarrhea,
stimulates liver function, dissolves stagnation.
Cooking time approx. 45 min
Calories p. portion: 308
2 portions
Allergens: GL

Quantity of ingredients:
Olive oil 1/2 teaspoon / 5g. (yes)
Onion (spring onion) 2 table spoons / 7g. (little)
Nutmeg 1 pinch / 0,3g. (recommended)
Parsley 1/2 bunch / 25g. (recommended)
Rice variety any 1/4 lbs - 4oz / 100g. (yes)
Carrot 5/8 lbs - 8oz / 250g. (recommended)
Basic recipe for a vegetable soup 1 cup / 280g. (recommended)
Fennel seeds ground 1/4 teaspoon / 1g. (recommended)
Basil (fresh) 1/2 teaspoon / 2g. (recommended)
Salt 1 pinch / 1g. (little)
Pepper (ground) 1 pinch / 0,3g. (little)
Parmesan 1 table spoon / 10g. (little)

Cooking instructions:
Heat the oil in a pan, fry the onions in a glassy and very soft manner. Add parsley, sauté briefly. Add rice, carrots and nutmeg, sauté briefly while stirring. Add the vegetable stock, season with fennel and basil, heat till it boils and cook for about 20 minutes until the rice and carrots are well. Stir from time to time and add some vegetable stock if necessary. The risotto should be slightly soupy. Just before the end of the cooking time mix in the white wine and simmer the risotto for a short while. Remove risotto from the heat, mix in Parmesan.

9.20 Celery and potato cream soup

Reduces blood pressure, strengthens immune system, promotes weight loss. Good to fight immunodeficiency, loss of appetite, flatulence, depressions, diabetes, diarrhea, improves digestion.
Cooking time approx. 45 min
Calories p. portion: 113
4 portions
Allergens: GL

Quantity of ingredients:
Olive oil 1 table spoon / 10g. (yes)
Onion white 1/2 piece / 25g. (little)
Basic recipe for a vegetable soup 3 cups / 700g. (recommended)
Potato 5/8 oz / 200g. (recommended)
Nutmeg 1 pinch / 0,5g. (recommended)
Ground 1 pinch / 0,5g. (yes)
Lemon peel 1/4 piece / 1g. (yes)
Créme fraiche cheese 2 table spoons / 20g. (yes)
Salt 1 pinch / 1g. (little)
Parsley 1 table spoon / 8g. (recommended)

Cooking instructions:
Heat the olive oil in a saucepan lightly. Fry the onions very gently in a mild heat. Pour with vegetable stock according to the basic recipe. Cover and cook for 15 minutes.
Add curd-cut potato, celery, nutmeg, cumin and lemon zest. Spice with salt and cook for 12 minutes. Potatoes and celery should be soft. Remove the lemon peel.
Puree the soup with crème fraiche using a blender. Season the soup with salt.
Arrange the soup in portions with the chopped parsley.

9.21 Celery juice

Mineral and vitamin rich, forces metabolism and dehydrating effect.
Cooking time approx. 5 min
Calories p. portion: 33
1 portions
Allergens: L

Quantity of ingredients:
Celery root 1/2 piece / 200g. (recommended)
Water 1 cup / 120g. (yes)
Salt 1 pinch / 0,5g. (little)

Cooking instructions:
Peel celeriac and cut into pieces and juice. Mix with water and salt as needed.

9.22 Celery salad with lemon and olive oil

Mineral and vitamin rich, forces metabolism and dehydrating effect.
Cooking time approx. 10 min
Calories p. portion: 402
1 portions
Allergens: L

Quantity of ingredients:
Celery root 1/2 piece / 200g. (recommended)
Lemon juice 1/2 piece / 10g. (yes)
Olive oil 4 table spoons / 40g. (yes)

Cooking instructions:
Peel celeriac and cut into pieces and rub. Serve with the lemon juice and olive oil.

9.23 Chicken in an ilalian style

Strengthens bone marrow, improves blood circulation, strengthens the muscles, antioxidativ. Basmati rice: To drain the body overweight and high blood pressure.
Cooking time approx. 1 hour
Calories p. portion: 410
4 portions
Allergens: M

Quantity of ingredients:
Olive oil 2 table spoons / 30g. (yes)
Chicken meat 1 piece (cut into 8 pieces) / 700g. (yes)
Garlic 3 cloves / 5g. (recommended)
Rosemary 1/2 teaspoon / 2g. (yes)
Salt 1 pinch / 1g. (little)
Pepper (ground) 1 pinch / 0,5g. (little)
Water 1 cup / 20g. (yes)
Rice Basmati 1 cup / 120g. (yes)
Water 6 cups / 400g. (yes)
Salt 1 pinch / 1g. (little)
Lettuce 1 piece / 300g. (yes)
Olive oil 2 table spoons / 20g. (yes)
Lemon juice 1/4 piece / 7g. (yes)
Mustard 1 pinch / 3g. (yes)
Salt 1 pinch / 1g. (little)
Honey 1 pinch / 2g. (yes)

Cooking instructions:
In a heavy pan (with lid) heat 1 tbsp of olive oil at low temperature. Add the chicken pieces and fry for a few minutes. Once they start to take on color, add the remaining 2 tablespoons of olive oil and garlic. Turn the chicken parts in the oil and sprinkle with rosemary, salt and pepper. Pour with a little water and heat till it boils. Reduce the heat, put on the lid and stew the chicken for 35 to 45 minutes.

In between, check again and again whether there is enough cooking water, and if necessary, add 1 to 2 tablespoons of water each time.

As soon as the meat comes off the bone, spread the chicken parts on the plates, deglaze the roast residue in the braised pan with a few tablespoons of water or wine and spread over the meat as a sauce.

In the meantime, cook the rice in a saucepan with (1:6) salted water, on a low heat.

Wash and spin the lettuce, finely chop and serve in a bowl. In a small bowl, mix the olive oil, lemon juice, mustard, salt and honey well and add to the salad and add it to the salad.

9.24 Chicken soup with egg yolk and parsley

Strengthens blood, strengthens bone marrow, reduces blood pressure, strengthens immune system. Parsley stimulates liver function, harmonizes liver and spleen, strengthens eyesight, detoxifying.
Cooking time approx. 10 min
Calories p. portion: 118
2 portions
Allergens: CL

Quantity of ingredients:
Basic recipe for a chicken soup (warming) 2 cup / 500g. (yes)
Chicken yolk 1 piece / 10g. (little)
Parsley 1 table spoon / 10g. (recommended)

Cooking instructions:
Cook the chicken broth according to the basic recipe.
Heat broth and bubble the egg yolk. Sprinkle the chopped parsley over it and let it rest for about 2 minutes. Drink in small sips.

9.25 Chicken soup with green spelt, parsley and sake

Strengthens blood, strengthens bone marrow, reduces blood pressure, strengthens immune system, stimulates liver function, detoxifying. Improves blood circulation, improves medication effect, stimulates appetite.
Cooking time approx. 1 1/2 hours
Calories p. portion: 150
2 portions
Allergens: AL

Quantity of ingredients:
Basic recipe for a chicken soup (warming) 2 cup / 500g. (yes)
Green spelt 4 table spoons / 30g. (yes)
Parsley 2 table spoons / 14g. (recommended)
Sake 1 dash / 2g. (yes)

Cooking instructions:
Cook the chicken broth according to the basic recipe. Add the ingredients in the soup and simmer 10 min.

9.26 Chicken with white turnips on rice

Strengthens bone marrow. Rice to drain the body at overweight and high blood pressure.
Cooking time approx. 45 min
Calories p. portion: 324
4 portions
Allergens: GL

Quantity of ingredients:
Butter organic 2 table spoons / 20g. (yes)
Olive oil 2 table spoons / 20g. (yes)
Onion white 1 piece / 60g. (little)
Turnips 4 pieces / 200g. (recommended)
Garlic 2 pieces / 3g. (recommended)
Basic recipe for a chicken soup (warming) 1 cup / 100g. (yes)
Parsley 2 table spoons / 15g. (recommended)
Salt 1 pinch / 1g. (little)
Olive oil 1 teaspoon / 4g. (yes)
Chicken meat 7/8 lbs / 400g. (yes)
Water 6 cups / 400g. (yes)
Rice Basmati 1 cup / 120g. (yes)

Cooking instructions:
In a heavy pot, heat the butter and the oil at low temperature. Add the onion, stir and simmer for about 20 minutes on very low heat until soft and golden brown. Add the chopped beets and the chopped garlic cloves and stir well. Add the chicken broth or water, add some salt and heat till it boils. Reduce the heat, put on the lid and simmer the beets for about 20 minutes. Look in between if there is still enough liquid in the pot, and if necessary, pour in a few tablespoons of chicken stock. At the end there should be very little liquid in the pot. Remove the lid and allow the remaining liquid to evaporate, stirring constantly.
In the meantime roast the finely chopped chicken pieces in a frying pan with a little oil. Finally, sprinkle with a little chilli and fry for another minute while constantly turning.
Serve the pieces of chicken, turnips and rice on the plates, spread the sauce over them and sprinkle with parsley immediately.
Cook the rice in the ratio of 6 cups of water: 1 cup of rice.
Small, fresh, untreated beets do not need to be peeled. Otherwise, peel beets and place in hot water for 10 minutes. This makes them easier to digest and lose some of their sharp, pungent odor. White turnips are rich in vitamin C, potassium and folic acid.

9.27 Coconut rice with cardamom

Nourishing and slightly warming. Diuretic, reduces blood glucose.
Supports urination. Stimulates liver function. Good to fight depressions.
Cooking time approx. 45 min
Calories p. portion: 266
4 portions
Allergens: GO

Quantity of ingredients:
Rice long grain rice 1 cup / 120g. (yes)
Water 6 cups / 400g. (yes)
Sugar cane sugar 1 table spoon / 10g. (little)
Cardamom 1 teaspoon / 2g. (recommended)
Ginger fresh 1/2 teaspoon / 2g. (recommended)
Butter organic 2 table spoons / 20g. (yes)
Coconut grated 2 table spoons / 16g. (yes)
Cashews 1 table spoon / 8g. (yes)
Raisins 1 table spoon / 8g. (yes)
Salt 1 pinch / 0,5g. (little)
Lemon 1/2 piece / 15g. (yes)
Pumpkin 3/4 lbs / 300g. (recommended)
Olive oil 2 table spoons / 20g. (yes)
Coriander 1 pinch / 0,2g. (recommended)
Pepper (ground) 1 pinch / 0,2g. (little)
Curry 1 pinch / 0,5g. (little)
Water 1/4 cup / 50g. (yes)
Salt 1 pinch / 0,5g. (little)
Parsley 1 table spoon / 8g. (recommended)
Cardamom 1 pinch / 0,2g. (recommended)
Turmeric (yellow root) 1 pinch / 0,2g. (recommended)

Cooking instructions:
Preparation: Soak long grain rice in cold water for 1 hour and drain.
Then: Heat fresh water till it boils; add some whole cane sugar, plenty
of ground cardamom or some cardamom pods, grated ginger and the
rice into the hot water and cook.

Separately: heat some butter in a hot pot; add grated coconut, cashews
and raisins; add the cooked rice and salt; pour lemon juice over it; mix
everything and let it pass for a few minutes.

Pumpkin vegetables: heat olive oil in a pan. Steam the pumpkin (cut in cubes), season with cilantro, pepper and curry, simmer with a little water, salt with sea salt, add chopped parsley with cardamom and turmeric, simmer on a small fire for about 10 minutes, depending on the pumpkin, the pumpkin should still be firm.

9.28 Compote from blueberries

Laxative, antibacterial effect. Warms stomach and spleen, improves blood circulation.
Cooking time approx. 10 min
Calories p. portion: 49
1 portions
Allergens:

Quantity of ingredients:
Blueberry 1/4 lbs - 4oz / 100g. (yes)
Water 1 cup / 120g. (yes)
Cinnamon ground 1 pinch / 0,1g. (recommended)
Lemon peel 1 pinch / 1g. (yes)
Sugar cane sugar 1 teaspoon / 3g. (little)

Cooking instructions:
Cook the blueberries gently and sprinkle with sugar, cinnamon and grated lemon zest.

9.29 Compote of pears

Pear benefits digestion, supports urination. Cocoa forces liver, strengthens the defense. Good to fight fungi infections.
Cooking time approx. 10 min
Calories p. portion: 122
4 portions
Allergens:

Quantity of ingredients:
Water 1 cup / 280g. (yes)
Pear 4 pieces / 800g. (recommended)
Anise (Common Fennel) 1/2 teaspoon / 1g. (recommended)
Vanilla pod 1 pinch / 1g. (recommended)
Cocoa 1 pinch / 1g. (yes)

Cooking instructions:
Boil pears (organic - with peel), aniseed, vanilla, chili soft. Sprinkle with cocoa.

9.30 Cottage cheese with steamed fruit

Good to fight loss of appetite, promotes digestion, supports urination.
Cooking time approx. 20 min
Calories p. portion: 214
2 portions
Allergens: G

Quantity of ingredients:
Cottage cheese 3/4 lbs / 300g. (yes)
Apple (sour) 1 piece / 100g. (recommended)
Pear 1 piece / 100g. (recommended)

Cooking instructions:
Wash apples and pears well, do not peel, and chop small. In a pot with steam filter, boil them al dente, remove and allow to cool down. Serve the cheese, spread the fruit on it.

9.31 Couscous Salad

prevents cancer, forcing spleen, promotes digestion, stimulates liver function, reduces blood pressure, strengthens immune system, reduces radiation damage, diuretic.
Cooking time approx. 25 min
Calories p. portion: 338
3 portions
Allergens: A

Quantity of ingredients:
Water 1 cup / 100g. (yes)
Olive oil 1 table spoon / 15g. (yes)
Couscous 5/8 oz / 200g. (yes)
Lemon juice 2 table spoons / 30g. (yes)
Lemon peel 1 teaspoon / 2g. (yes)
Tomato 2 pieces / 80g. (recommended)
Cucumber 1/4 lbs - 4oz / 100g. (recommended)
Carrot 1/4 lbs - 4oz / 100g. (recommended)
Parsley 1 Bunch / 100g. (recommended)
Chives 1 Bunch / 100g. (yes)
Peppermint 3 twigs / 30g. (yes)

Cooking instructions:
Boil in a small saucepan 250 ml. water with salt and 1 tablespoon olive oil. Add the couscous, take the stove in the front and let it swell covered

for 5 minutes. Put the couscous back on the stove and let it simmer for about 2 minutes with gentle stirring. If necessary, add 1 - 3 tbsp of hot water.
Mix the couscous with lemon juice, chopped lemon peel and 1 tbsp oil, season with salt and pepper and leave to set.
Add couscous with tomatoes, cucumber, parsley (all diced), carrots (grated), chives and mint (finely chopped). Season the couscous salad with lemon juice, salt and pepper.

9.32 Cranberry juice

Antibacterial, good to fight loss of appetite, arteriosclerosis, bladder infections, diarrhea, colds. Antipyretic, against free radicals, gout, diuretic, stomach ulcers, oral mucosa inflammation, rheumatism.
Cooking time approx. 5 min
Calories p. portion: 43
1 portions
Allergens:

Quantity of ingredients:
Cranberries 2 table spoons / 25g. (recommended)
Water 1 cup / 125g. (yes)
Honey 1 table spoon / 10g. (yes)

Cooking instructions:
Mix the cranberries with a little water with the blender to a pulp. Add the remaining water and sweeten with the honey.

9.33 Cucumber soup

Diuretic, detoxifying, suppresses conversion of sugar into fat, lowers cholesterol, prevents cancer, promotes digestion, diaphoretic, dries out, good to fight yeast infections.
Cooking time approx. 20 min
Calories p. portion: 96
4 portions
Allergens: M

Quantity of ingredients:
Olive oil 2 table spoons / 35g. (yes)
Cucumber 2 pieces / 400g. (recommended)
Water 2 cup / 500g. (yes)
Sage 3 leaves / 3g. (yes)
Mustard 1/2 teaspoon / 0,5g. (yes)

Coriander 1 pinch / 1g. (recommended)
Cardamom 1 pinch / 1g. (recommended)
Salt 1 pinch / 1g. (little)

Cooking instructions:
Heat oil and roast short the small cucumbers. Add Mustard seeds, coriander, cardamom and salt. Add water. Simmer for 10-15 min. Puree and decorate with fresh chopped sage.

9.34 Duck soup with algae

Strengthens blood, forcing spleen, Supports urination. reduces blood pressure, strengthens immune system, prevents cancer, reduces radiation damage, detoxifying and stimulating the immune system.
Cooking time approx. 3-4 hours
Calories p. portion: 664
4 portions
Allergens: E

Quantity of ingredients:
Duck (slaughtered) 2 cup / 1000g. (yes)
Garlic 2 cloves / 4g. (recommended)
Onion white 1 piece / 50g. (little)
Ginger fresh 1/2 teaspoon / 2g. (recommended)
Curcuma 1/2 teaspoon / 2g. (yes)
Carrot 2 pieces / 120g. (recommended)
Lemon 2 cup / 15g. (yes)
Cinnamon ground 1/4 stick / 3g. (recommended)
Star anise 2 pieces / 2g. (yes)
Fish sauce 1 teaspoon / 3g. (yes)
Soy sauce 2 teaspoons / 6g. (yes)
Juniper berry 4 pieces / 2g. (yes)
Coriander (fresh) 1/4 Bunch / 100g. (recommended)
Wakame 1/4 lbs / 100g. (yes)

Cooking instructions:
This soup tastes better, the next day.
1. Place the duck with its innards (with the exception of the liver), the cleaned vegetables and all the spices (a little coriander leaves retained) in a large saucepan and cover with water. Bring to the boil and simmer for about 2 hours.

2. Trigger the meat cleanly, parry the innards, and cut into accurate,

bite-sized slices or cubes. Pour over some broth and set aside. Put the bones and skin back into the soup in the pot, cook everything for another 3 - 4 hours, until the vegetables begins to dissolve.

3. Degrease the soup, which works best if left cold overnight and the fat on the surface solidifies. Heat the soup again and drive through a sieve.

4. To serve, chop the algae and simmer for 5 minutes in the soup, add the meat and reheat.

5. Season the soup with fish sauce and lemon juice and sprinkle with the remaining cilantro.

9.35 Fennel and potato gratin

Reduces inflammation, improves blood circulation, improves digestion, supports urination, lowers cholesterol, good to fight loss of appetite, flatulence, inflammatory bowel disease, heartburn. Forcing spleen, improves blood circulation.
Cooking time approx. 1 1/2 hours
Calories p. portion: 147
2 portions
Allergens: CGL

Quantity of ingredients:
Fennel 5/8 oz / 200g. (recommended)
Potato 1/4 lbs - 4oz / 125g. (recommended)
Basic recipe for a vegetable soup 1/2 cup / 100g. (recommended)
Butter organic 1 teaspoon / 3g. (yes)
Rice flour 2 teaspoons / 6g. (yes)
Cream sour 10% 1 teaspoon / 3g. (yes)
Salt 1 pinch / 1g. (little)
Sugar cane sugar 1 pinch / 1g. (little)
Chicken yolk 1 piece / 10g. (little)
Pepper Cayenne 1 pinch / 0,5g. (little)
Nutmeg 1 pinch / 0,5g. (recommended)
Parsley 1 teaspoon / 2g. (recommended)
Chives 1 teaspoon / 3g. (yes)
Parmesan 1 teaspoon / 3g. (little)
Butter organic 1 teaspoon / 3g. (yes)

Cooking instructions:
Cook peeled potatoes and then let cool. Wash the fennel, cut off the stems and remove any outer leaves.
Hold back fennel greens and add it to the sauce with the other herbs later.
Steam the fennel tubers for about 15 - 20 minutes.
Then cut the potatoes and fennel into slices and place in layers in a greased baking dish.
Bring the liquid of fennel broth to the boil and bind it with flour.
Season with sea salt, cayenne pepper, sugar, nutmeg and sour cream.
Allow to cool and alloy with egg yolk.
Spread the sauce over the casserole, sprinkle with parmesan and finely chopped parsley and chives. Bake at 200 °C / 392 °F in the oven for half an hour.

9.36 Figs with mozzarella and honey

Promotes digestion, reduces inflammation, bloating and nausea, relaxing and reassuring, relieves pain, detoxifying, blood stilling, forcing spleen and digestive system, detoxifying, bactericide.
Cooking time approx. 10 min
Calories p. portion: 415
1 portions
Allergens: GO

Quantity of ingredients:
Fig 4 pieces / 100g. (yes)
Mozzarella 1 piece / 50g. (yes)
Basil (fresh) 1/2 bunch / 50g. (recommended)
Honey 2 table spoons / 24g. (yes)
Pepper (ground) 1 pinch / 0,1g. (little)
Grapeseed oil 1 table spoon / 12g. (yes)
Vinegar Aceto Balsamico white 1 table spoon / 12g. (yes)

Cooking instructions:
Quarter fresh figs, dice buffalo mozzarella, pluck basil leaves.
Mix a dressing with light balsamic vinegar, grapeseed oil and honey and season to taste.
Place the figs on the edge of the appropriate plate. Spread the mozzarella cubes and season with black pepper. Spread whole or roughly sliced basil leaves over it and moisten with the marinade.
Spiced pizza bread goes perfectly with it.

9.37 Fish soup with rosemary

Promotes spleen and liver, reduces blood pressure, strengthens immune system, prevents cancer, reduces radiation damage, has little cholesterol and is protein rich, improves blood circulation, increases appetite. Antioxidant, forcing spleen, dissolves stagnation.
Cooking time approx. 30 min
Calories p. portion: 271
4 portions
Allergens: DLO

Quantity of ingredients:
Basic recipe for a fish soup 2 cup / 500g. (yes)
Rosemary 1/2 bunch / 7g. (yes)
Onion (spring onion) 1 piece / 20g. (little)
Olive oil 2 table spoons / 35g. (yes)
Fish pieces mixed (fresh water) 5/8 lbs - 8oz / 250g. (recommended)
Carrot 1 piece / 120g. (recommended)
Parsnip 1 piece / 180g. (recommended)
Celery root 1 slice / 20g. (recommended)
Salt 1 pinch / 1g. (little)
Peppercorns 2 pieces / 1g. (little)
Garlic 1 clove / 3g. (recommended)

Cooking instructions:
Fry the onion and garlic in oil. Add fish broth. Add diced carrots, parsnips and celery. Season with salt and peppercorns. Simmer the soup on a low heat for 25 minutes.
Wash the fish, drizzle with lemon juice, divide into pieces and add to the soup with the pink rosemary. Cook for 5 min on low heat.
Add the chives and parsley and season the soup with the salt.

9.38 Fried asparagus with rocket

Diuretic, improves blood circulation, prevents cancer, stimulates digestion, forcing spleen, promotes weight loss. Good to fight immunodeficiency, loss of appetite, arteriosclerosis, flatulence, bladder weakness, anemia, high blood pressure, depressions, diabetes.
Cooking time approx. 15 min
Calories p. portion: 149
3 portions
Allergens: G

Quantity of ingredients:
Butter organic 1 table spoon / 20g. (yes)
Asparagus (green or white) 1,1 lbs / 500g. (recommended)
Pepper (ground) 1 pinch / 0,5g. (little)
Salt 1 pinch / 1g. (little)
Lemon 1/4 piece / 12g. (yes)
Rucola 2 handful / 30g. (yes)
Potato 3/4 lbs / 300g. (recommended)

Cooking instructions:
Melt a piece of butter in a hot pan; cut the peeled asparagus into pieces of 3 to 4 cm, fry for about 10 minutes until tender, but crisp. Sprinkle with freshly ground pepper, salt, add a few drops of lemon juice or finely grated lemon zest, finely shredded rucola leaves.
Cook the potatoes in plenty of salted water, then peel.

9.39 Grated apple

Eat 3 times a day - Apple (sour) scraped and brown is stuffing. Relieves diarrhea.
Cooking time approx. 10 min
Calories p. portion: 120
1 portions
Allergens:

Quantity of ingredients:
Apple (sour) 1 piece / 200g. (recommended)

Cooking instructions:
Peel apple and grate as fine as possible. Leave for at least 5 minutes until it turns brown.

9.40 Grilled salmon steaks with cauliflower and potatoes

Improves digestion, regenerates skin, supports urination, lowers cholesterol, supports digestion.
Cooking time approx. 30 min
Calories p. portion: 330
4 portions
Allergens: D

Quantity of ingredients:
Garlic 1 clove / 1g. (recommended)
Onion (shallot) 1/2 piece / 5g. (little)
Lemon juice 1 dach / 1g. (yes)
Salt 1 pinch / 1g. (little)
Cauliflower 1 piece / 500g. (little)
Olive oil 2 table spoons / 20g. (yes)
Garlic 1 clove / 1g. (recommended)
Water 2/3 cup / g. (yes)
Parsley 2 table spoons / 15g. (recommended)
Potato 1,1 lbs / 500g. (recommended)
Salt 1 pinch / 1g. (little)
Salmon 4 pieces (steaks) / 500g. (yes)
Lemon 1/2 piece / 2g. (yes)

Cooking instructions:
Garlic shallots mixture:
Finely squeeze the garlic, finely chop the shallots, add a dash of lemon juice and salt and stir. Mix with a little oil to a paste.

Cauliflower:
Cut the cauliflower into pieces.
Heat the oil in a heavy saucepan and fry the crushed garlic for a short time.
Add the cauliflower pieces and turn in the oil. Add a little water and cook until the cauliflower is firm. Strain the cauliflower and cook the remaining water until a thick sauce remains. Add the cauliflower and crush it roughly with a wooden spoon. Add the chopped parsley and salt.

Potatoes:
Cook the potato in a saucepan with plenty of water, strain and peel.

Salmon Steak:
Preheat the oven at about 180°C/356°F. Rub in the salmon slices with the garlic-scarlet mixture and grill as close as possible to the heat source for 4 to 8 minutes from both sides. You are done when the meat is easy to divide when you pierce with a fork.

Serve and sprinkle with lemon slices and the chopped parsley.

9.41 Grilled tofu with rice noodles, spinach and sugar snaps

Reduces flatulence. Supports urination, detoxifying. Good to fight blood circulation disorders. Strengthens gastrointestinal function, expands blood vessels, stimulates appetite. Promotes bowel movement, improves blood circulation.
Cooking time approx. 30 min
Calories p. portion: 327
4 portions
Allergens: E

Quantity of ingredients:
Sake 1/3 cup / 85g. (yes)
Sugar cane sugar 1 table spoon / 7g. (little)
Garlic 5 cloves / 7g. (recommended)
Onion (spring onion) 3 pieces / 60g. (little)
Ginger fresh 1 inch / 5g. (recommended)
Rapeseed oil 2 table spoons / 20g. (yes)
Spinach 2 handful / 30g. (recommended)
Peas, green 7/8 lbs / 400g. (recommended)
Water 1 table spoon / g. (yes)
Rice noodles 1 package / 250g. (yes)
Water 4 cup / g. (yes)
Basil 1 table spoon / 3g. (recommended)
Soy Tofu 1,1 lbs / 500g. (little)

Cooking instructions:
In a medium bowl mix together: Tamari souce, rice wine, sugar, crushed garlic, spring onion, grated ginger, chopped basil and the rapeseed oil. Add the tofu and leave in the marinade for at least 1 hour. Cover the mangetout peas in a pan with a little water, lightly simmer 5 min. Add the spinach and steam again 3 min.

Cook the rice noodles according to manufacturer's instructions, drain, rinse again with warm water and drain.
Preheat the grill or oven grill, grill the tofu for 5 minutes on both sides and set aside.
Arrange the pasta on the plates, divide the vegetables all around and place the tofu over the noodles. Douse with the marinade.

9.42 Halibut with tomato and garlic sauce

Promotes digestion, helps to digest fat, supports urination, reduces blood pressure, good to fight rheumatism, flatulence, bladder weakness, anemia, high blood pressure, depressions, diabetes, diarrhea. Valuable omega-3 fatty acids.
Cooking time approx. 45 min
Calories p. portion: 319
5 portions
Allergens: D

Quantity of ingredients:
Rice variety any 1 cup / 120g. (yes)
Water 6 cups / 240g. (yes)
Salt 1 pinch / 1g. (little)
Halibut (Flatfish) 2,2 lbs / 800g. (yes)
Salt 1 pinch / 1g. (little)
Pepper (ground) 1 pinch / 0,5g. (little)
Lemon juice 1 dach / 2g. (yes)
Bay leaf 2 pieces / 2g. (recommended)
Lemon 1 piece / 30g. (yes)
Garlic 8 pieces / 10g. (recommended)
Thyme dried 1 table spoon / 5g. (yes)
Olives 0,2 lbs / 75g. (yes)
Tomato 4 pieces / 200g. (recommended)
Salt 1 pinch / 1g. (little)
Pepper (ground) 1 pinch / 0,5g. (little)

Cooking instructions:
Cook rice with salted water (1:3).
Rinse the fish under running cold water, dab with kitchen paper and rub with salt, pepper and lemon juice.
Place the fish fillets in a casserole dish with pieces of bay leaf.

Wash the lemon hot and cut into slices, peel and halve the garlic.
Sprinkle the olives and the thyme over them.
Brew the tomatoes with hot water, skin and chop.

Mix all ingredients, season with salt and pepper and distribute around the fish.

Cook everything at 200°C/392°F for about 20 minutes.
Serve with the rice.

9.43 Japanese algae soup

Reduces blood pressure, strengthens immune system, prevents cancer, reduces radiation damage. Promotes digestion. Detoxifying and stimulates the immune system.
Cooking time approx. 20 min
Calories p. portion: 47
3 portions
Allergens:

Quantity of ingredients:
Wakame 1 oz / 25g. (yes)
Water 2 cup / 450g. (yes)
Onion (shallot) 1-2 pcs. / 30g. (little)
Radish (white, green, purple-red) 1/8 lbs - 2oz / 50g. (yes)
Carrot 2 pieces / 180g. (recommended)
Miso 2 table spoons / 20g. (yes)
Parsley 2 table spoons / 20g. (recommended)
Onion (spring onion) 1 table spoon (sliced)

Cooking instructions:
Soak wakame in water for a few minutes, remove and bring the water to the boil. Add finely chopped onions and wakame, radishes and carrots, cut into thin strips, and simmer for another 10 minutes. Dissolve miso in a little cooled cooking water and add it at the end. Sprinkle with parsley and spring onions.

9.44 Mango banana yoghurt drink ice cold

Good to fight loss of appetite, oral mucosa inflammation. Regulates gastrointestinal function, chronic constipation. Prevents cancer. Diuretic, forcing spleen.
Cooking time approx. 5 min
Calories p. portion: 121
2 portions
Allergens: G

Quantity of ingredients:
Mango juice 1/2 cup / 100g. (recommended)
Yogurt (natural, 1.5% fat) 1/4 lbs - 4oz / 100g. (yes)
Mineral water 1/2 cup / 100g. (yes)
Banana 1/2 piece / 150g. (recommended)
Acerola fruit nectar or powder 1 teaspoon / 2g. (recommended)

Cooking instructions:
Mix all the ingredients and 2-3 ice cubes in a blender.

9.45 Marinated cod on pumpkin puree

Reduces inflammation, improves digestion, promotes spleen, lung, stomach and kidneys, diuretic, reduces blood glucose, good to fight constipation and flatulence, dissolves stagnation.
Cooking time approx. 2 hours
Calories p. portion: 202
4 portions
Allergens: DG

Quantity of ingredients:
Potato 6 pieces / 400g. (recommended)
Pumpkin 5/8 oz / 200g. (recommended)
Onion white 1 piece / 50g. (little)
Oregano dried 1/2 teaspoon / 1g. (recommended)
Lemon juice 1/2 piece / 15g. (yes)
Salt 1 pinch / 1g. (little)
Pepper (ground) 1 pinch / 0,3g. (little)
Créme fraiche cheese 2 table spoons / 30g. (yes)
Yogurt (natural, 1.5% fat) 3/8 lbs - 6oz / 150g. (yes)
Oregano dried 1/4 teaspoon / 1g. (recommended)
Basil (fresh) 1/2 teaspoon / 2g. (recommended)
Cod 3/4 lbs / 300g. (yes)
Salt 1 pinch / 1g. (little)
Pepper (ground) 1 pinch / 0,3g. (little)
Olive oil 1 teaspoon / 3g. (yes)

Cooking instructions:
Mix yoghurt with oregano, basil and thyme. Wash the fish fillets, pat dry, place in a flat shape and pour over the marinade. Leave 2 hours in refrigerator.

Cook the potatoes in salted water until soft and peel.

Sauté the onion in oil until glassy, add the diced pumpkin and cook for about 10 min. Add oregano, lemon juice, salt, pepper and creme fraiche and puree with the blender.

Remove fish fillets from the marinade, drain, pat dry and salt. Coat a coated grill pan with 2 teaspoons of oil. Roast the fish fillets on both sides for 3 - 4 minutes and arrange with the potatoes on the pumpkin puree.

9.46 Marinated courgette with smoked tofu

Diuretic, reduces flatulence, good to fight chronic diarrhea, stomach bleeding, improves digestion, relaxing and reassuring.
Cooking time approx. 30 min
Calories p. portion: 132
2 portions
Allergens: EL

Quantity of ingredients:
Zucchini 7/8 lbs / 400g. (recommended)
Salt 1 pinch / 1g. (little)
Lemon juice 2 table spoons / 15g. (yes)
Basic recipe for a vegetable soup 2 table spoons / 30g. (recommended)
Olive oil 1 table spoon / 10g. (yes)
Basil 2 table spoons / 10g. (recommended)
Oregano fresh 1/2 teaspoon / 2g. (recommended)
Peppermint 1 teaspoon / 4g. (yes)
Capers in olive oil 1 table spoon / 8g. (yes)
Lemon peel 1/2 teaspoon / 2g. (yes)
Soy Tofu smoked 1/4 lbs - 4oz / 100g. (yes)

Cooking instructions:
Preheat the oven to 200°C/392°F (circulating air 180°C/356°F).
Cover a baking tray with baking paper and place the zucchini next to each other. Cook zucchini in preheated oven for 5 minutes, turn over and cook for another 5-6 minutes.
Mix the lemon juice, vegetable stock and oil with the whisk. Stir in basil, oregano, mint, chopped capers and grated lemon peel. Season the marinade with salt.
Mix the hot zucchini with the marinade and let cool.
Arrange marinated zucchini with smoked tofu cubes.

9.47 Melanzani with olive oil and turmeric

improves blood circulation, reduces inflammation, relieves pain, promotes digestion, helps to digest fat, supports urination, reduces blood pressure.
Cooking time approx. 30 min
Calories p. portion: 432
2 portions
Allergens: A

Quantity of ingredients:
Aubergine 2 pieces / 300g. (recommended)
Olive oil 4 table spoons / 60g. (yes)
Tomato 4 pieces / 200g. (recommended)
Turmeric (yellow root) 1/2 teaspoon / 1g. (recommended)
Ground 1 pinch / 1g. (yes)
Salt 1 pinch / 1g. (little)
White bread (wheat bread) 4 slices / 80g. (little)

Cooking instructions:
Cut the melanzani into slices and spread them with the tomatoes on a baking tray. Sprinkle with olive oil and then with turmeric, caraway and salt. Bake them in the tube 20 min.
Serve with the white bread.

9.48 Milk rice vanilla - with cherries

Little laxative, improves blood circulation, reduces inflammation, moisturizer dry skin. Strengthens spleen and stomach, strengthens the muscles. Antioxidant.
Cooking time approx. 20 min
Calories p. portion: 394
4 portions
Allergens: GO

Quantity of ingredients:
Cow's milk (1.5% fat) 3,3 lbs / 1400g. (yes)
Rice round grain 5/8 oz / 200g. (yes)
Pudding powder vanilla 1 package / 5g. (yes)
Cherry compote 5/8 oz / 200g. (yes)
Acai powder 2 teaspoons / 6g. (recommended)
Sugar white 1 table spoon / 9g. (little)
Salt 1 pinch / 1g. (little)

Cooking instructions:
Put milk in a saucepan and heat till it boil. Add the rice and remove from the heat. Leave 10 min. Put again on a small flame, add a pinch of salt and about 2 tablespoons of sugar. Add the packet of vanilla pudding. Carefully, with a small cooker setting, bring to the boil while stirring.

Pour the juice from the cherries.

Depending on your hunger, place the rice on a plate, arrange the cherries nicely and sprinkle 1-2 teaspoons of acai powder over the cherries with a powdered sugar sieve.

9.49 Noodles with turkeymeat and pineapple

Solves bile-, kidney- and bladder stones, provides Vitamin C, strengthens blood, strengthens bone marrow, reduces inflammation, supports urination.
Cooking time approx. 45 min
Calories p. portion: 292
4 portions
Allergens: ACGL

Quantity of ingredients:
Noodles (whole grain) with egg 5/8 oz / 200g. (yes)
Pineapple 5/8 oz / 200g. (yes)
Water 1/2 cup / 50g. (yes)
Turkey breast meat 5/8 oz / 200g. (yes)
Rapeseed oil 1 table spoon / 12g. (yes)
Garlic 1 piece / 2g. (recommended)
Basic recipe for a vegetable soup 1/2 cup / 100g. (recommended)
Cow's milk (whole milk 3.5% fat) 2/3 cup / 180g. (yes)
Fresh cheese 0,2 lbs / 75g. (yes)
Curry 3 teaspoons / 6g. (little)
Salt 1 pinch / 1g. (little)
Pepper (ground) 1 pinch / 0,5g. (little)
Pomegranate 1 piece / 300g. (yes)
Coconut flakes 1 table spoon / 6g. (little)

Cooking instructions:
Cook the noodles in salt water. Cut the pineapple into cubes and leave for 5 min. to simmer in water. Cut the meat sliced in strips and roast themin the oil. Add the chopped garlic and the pineapple sliced. Add about 50 ml of the ananas juice and stir in the vegetable broth. Add the

milk and the fresh cheese, then stir well until the fresh cheese is completely dissolved. Now add the curry and simmer for a few minutes until a creamy consistency is reached. Season with salt and pepper. Now add the noodles in the finished sauce. Cut the pomegranate and release the seeds. Distribute as many kernels on the dressed noodles. Whoever likes it can spread coconut chips over it.

9.50 Noodles with vegetable and tomato sauce

Protects the digestive system. Detoxifying, Good to fight loss of appetite, flatulence, inflammatory bowel disease, obesity, gout, stomach ulcers, stomach cramps, rheumatism, heartburn, twelffinger intestinal ulcers, promotes digestion, helps to digest fat.
Cooking time approx. 45 min
Calories p. portion: 562
2 portions
Allergens: ACG

Quantity of ingredients:
Tomato 1/4 lbs - 4oz / 125g. (recommended)
Carrot 1 piece / 80g. (recommended)
Zucchini 1 piece / 80g. (recommended)
Olive oil 1 table spoon / 15g. (yes)
Onion (shallot) 1 piece / 20g. (little)
Oregano dried 1 pinch / 1g. (recommended)
Salt 1 pinch / 1g. (little)
Pepper (ground) 1 pinch / 0,2g. (little)
Noodles (wheat) with egg 5/8 oz / 200g. (yes)
Olive oil 1 table spoon / 10g. (yes)
Créme fraiche cheese 2 table spoons / 30g. (yes)

Cooking instructions:
Boil the tomatoes with a little water, drain and collect the juice, cut the tomatoes into pieces.
Roughly grate zucchini and carrot. Heat olive oil in a pot. Steam shallots very soft. Add tomatoes, season with oregano, salt and pepper. Simmer tomatoes to a thick sauce.
Bring plenty of salted water to boil, cook the wholegrain noodles until firm. In the cooking time of the pasta, heat in a pan olive oil. Fry the carrots while stirring, lightly salt. Add zucchini, sauté briefly while stirring. The vegetables should be soft with a bite.
Drain pasta, mix with créme fraiche, season with salt and pepper. Garnish with the tomato sauce.

9.51 Oatmeal soup with spring onion and carrots

Reduces blood pressure, strengthens immune system, prevents cancer, reduces radiation damage, stimulates digestion, reduces pain, stimulates appetite, dissolves stagnation.
Cooking time approx. 30 min
Calories p. portion: 135
3 portions
Allergens: AG

Quantity of ingredients:
Oat 6 table spoons / 48g. (yes)
Carrot 2 pieces / 200g. (recommended)
Butter organic 1 table spoon / 15g. (yes)
Nutmeg 1 pinch / 1g. (recommended)
Lovage 1 stem / 15g. (recommended)
Onion (spring onion) 2 pieces / 40g. (little)
Water 2 cup / 480g. (yes)

Cooking instructions:
Roast the oats in butter, add salt and spices, pour in water and heat till it boils. After 10 min. add the grated carrots and lovage, cook for 10 minutes. Finely add chopped onion.

9.52 Oven potatoes with celery-curd cheese (quark)

Promotes spleen, reduces Inflammation, improves digestion, regenerates skin, supports urination, lowers cholesterol.
Cooking time approx. 30 min
Calories p. portion: 304
2 portions
Allergens: GL

Quantity of ingredients:
Celery root 3 oz / 80g. (recommended)
Basic recipe for a vegetable soup 1/2 cup / 100g. (recommended)
Ground caraway 1 pinch / 0,2g. (recommended)
Lemon peel 1/2 teaspoon / 1g. (yes)

Salt 1 pinch / 1g. (little)
Pepper (ground) 1 pinch / 0,2g. (little)
Lemon juice 1 teaspoon / 3g. (yes)
Curd cheese 20% 5/8 oz / 200g. (yes)
Créme fraiche cheese 1/2 teaspoon / 5g. (yes)
Potato 6 pieces / 400g. (recommended)
Olive oil 2 teaspoons / 5g. (yes)
Salt 1 pinch / 1g. (little)

Cooking instructions:
Celery-curd cheese:
Mix celery with vegetable broth according to basic recipe, caraway and lemon peel. Cook for about 8 minutes until the celery is soft and the vegetable broth almost evaporated. Mix the celery vegetable broth with the lemon juice, finely, and stir until smooth. Season with salt and pepper.

Baked potatoes:
Preheat oven to 200 °C / 400 °F.
Brush the potatoes well, halve them, and place them on a baking tray with the cut surface facing up. Lightly salt the surfaces and sprinkle with oil. Fry the potatoes in the oven for about 25 minutes.
Serve the celery plug to the potatoes.

9.53 Pancakes with spinach and parmesan

Promotes bowel movement, improves blood circulation, forcing spleen and bowel, strengthens immune system, good to fight loss of appetite, flatulence, high blood pressure, depressions, diabetes, constipation, inflammatory bowel disease
Cooking time approx. 25 min
Calories p. portion: 330
6 portions
Allergens: ACGL

Quantity of ingredients:
Wholemeal flour 1/4 lbs - 4oz / 100g. (recommended)
Wheat flour 1/4 lbs - 4oz / 100g. (yes)
Chicken egg 4 pieces / 200g. (little)
Cow's milk (whole milk 3.5% fat) 1 1/2 cups / 400g. (yes)
Salt 1 pinch / 1g. (little)
Sunflower oil 1 table spoon / 15g. (yes)
Olive oil 1 table spoon / 15g. (yes)

Onion white 1 piece / 50g. (little)
Parsley 1/2 bunch / 80g. (recommended)
Basic recipe for a vegetable soup 1/2 cup / 150g. (recommended)
Basil (fresh) 1/4 teaspoon / 1g. (recommended)
Nutmeg 1 pinch / 0,3g. (recommended)
Créme fraiche cheese 2 table spoons / 45g. (yes)
Spinach 1,3 lbs / 600g. (recommended)
Salt 1 pinch / 1g. (little)
Pepper (ground) 1 pinch / 0,1g. (little)
Parmesan 1/8 lbs - 2oz / 60g. (little)

Cooking instructions:
Stir flour, eggs and milk and a pinch of salt with the whisk until smooth.
From the dough, fry pancakes crispy brown on both sides.

Heat oil in a small saucepan. Fry the finely chopped onion until tender.
Stir in chopped parsley, sauté briefly. Add the vegetable broth
according to the basic recipe, season with basil and nutmeg. Cover and
simmer for 15 minutes, add creme fraiche and finely puree.
Cook the washed, drizzled spinach with a little salt in a closed pan over
a moderate heat in 3 minutes, drain in a sieve and cut into small pieces.
Add the spinach to the sauce, heat briefly. Add parmesan in the mix.
Fill the pancakes with the cream spinach.

9.54 Pear compote

Promotes digestion, supports urination.
Cooking time approx. 20 min
Calories p. portion: 100
3 portions
Allergens:
Quantity of ingredients:
Water 1 1/2 cups / 240g. (yes)
Pear 4 / 500g. (recommended)

Cooking instructions:
Halve organic pears. Cores and skin can be used. Pear in the pot and
add water. Simmer for up to 20 minutes until pears are tender.

9.55 Polenta with fried egg

Calms nerves, forcing spleen and stomach, lets urine and bile juice flow, prevents cancer, forcing spleen, improves blood circulation, encourages growth, dissolves stagnation.
Cooking time approx. 15 min
Calories p. portion: 410
2 portions
Allergens: CG

Quantity of ingredients:
Water 1 1/2 cups / 200g. (yes)
Corn Grease (Polenta) 1 cup / 120g. (yes)
Ginger fresh 1 pinch / 0,5g. (recommended)
Butter organic 1/2 teaspoon / 2g. (yes)
Pepper (ground) 1 pinch / 0,2g. (little)
Nutmeg 1 pinch / 0,2g. (recommended)
Salt 1 pinch / 0,5g. (little)
Lemon juice 1 dach / 1g. (yes)
Pepper powder (hot) 1 pinch / 0,3g. (yes)
Chicken egg 4 pieces / 250g. (little)
Chives 2 table spoons / 14g. (yes)

Cooking instructions:
Stir in a saucepan with hot water polenta and a little ginger; swell until the polenta is cooked.
Add a piece of butter, pepper, nutmeg, salt, a few drops of lemon, a pinch of rose paprika.
Put the polenta in a fireproof bowl.
Put 1 fried egg per person on top; bake in the oven for a few minutes, so that the egg yolk is still liquid.
Sprinkle with ground pepper, finely chopped chives and a little salt.

9.56 Potato cream with herbs and fresh cheese

Good to fight loss of appetite, constipation, bloating and nausea.
Improves digestion, supports urination, prevents cancer, forcing spleen, dissolves stagnation, relaxing and reassuring.
Cooking time approx. 25 min
Calories p. portion: 217
2 portions
Allergens: G

Quantity of ingredients:
Potato (mealy) 5/8 lbs - 8oz / 250g. (recommended)
Fresh cheese 3 oz / 80g. (yes)
Yogurt (natural, 1.5% fat) 2 table spoons / 45g. (yes)
Chives 1/2 bunch / 50g. (yes)
Basil (fresh) 1 teaspoon / 4g. (recommended)
Parsley 1 teaspoon / 4g. (recommended)
Dill 1/2 teaspoon / 2g. (recommended)
Salt 1 pinch / 1g. (little)
Black caraway 1 pinch / 0,5g. (yes)
Pepper (ground) 1 pinch / 0,5g. (little)

Cooking instructions:
Softly steam the potatoes in the pan, peel them and press through the potato press.
Mix cream cheese, yoghurt and herbs under the potatoes, season with salt, crushed black cumin and pepper.

9.57 Potato gnocchi with vegetables and basil sauce

Strengthens immune system, promotes weight loss. Good to fight immunodeficiency, loss of appetite, flatulence, high blood pressure. Relaxing and reassuring.
Cooking time approx. 1 hour
Calories p. portion: 167
4 portions
Allergens: ACGL

Quantity of ingredients:
Potato 5/8 lbs - 8oz / 250g. (recommended)
Wheat flour 1 oz / 25g. (yes)
Wheat semolina 1/2 oz / 15g. (yes)
Chicken yolk 1 piece / 20g. (little)
Nutmeg 1 pinch / 0,2g. (recommended)
Basic recipe for a vegetable soup 1 cup / 250g. (recommended)
Celery root 1/8 lbs - 2oz / 50g. (recommended)
Lemon peel 1/2 teaspoon / 2g. (yes)
Ginger fresh 1/2 teaspoon / 2g. (recommended)
Nutmeg 1 pinch / 0,2g. (recommended)
Basil (fresh) 1 Bunch / 125g. (recommended)
Créme fraiche cheese 1 table spoon / 20g. (yes)

Salt 1 pinch / 1g. (little)
Pepper (ground) 1 pinch / 0,2g. (little)
Carrot 1/4 lbs - 4oz / 100g. (recommended)
Zucchini 1/4 lbs - 4oz / 100g. (recommended)
Cauliflower 1/4 lbs - 4oz / 100g. (little)
Broccoli 1/4 lbs - 4oz / 100g. (recommended)
Salt 1 pinch / 1g. (little)

Cooking instructions:
Steam the potatoes gently, peel and pass hot through the potato press.
Process the hot potatoes with flour, semolina, egg, nutmeg and salt to a
smooth dough. Let dough rest for 3o minutes.
Make small rolls (2 cm) out of the dough with flour-dusted hands, cut off
1 cm thin slices. To create the typical gnocchi shape, gently dab the
dough pieces with your thumb. Leave the gnocchi in lightly boiling
salted water for 6 - 8 minutes. Lift the gnocchi out of the pot with the
skimmer.

Heat the vegetable stock till it boils. Add diced celery, grated lemon
peel, finely chopped ginger and 1 pinch of nutmeg. Cover and simmer
for about 10 minutes. Using the blender, puree the vegetable broth,
celery, chopped basil and créme fraiche into a smooth sauce. Season
with salt and nutmeg.

Cut carrots, zucchini, cauliflower and broccoli into small pieces and
cook covered in a sieve over steam for 8 minutes until firm.
Heat the sauce again and add to the vegetables and arrange over the
gnocchi.

9.58 Potato-basil soup

Reduces inflammation, improves digestion, supports urination, lowers
cholesterol, reduces blood pressure, strengthens immune system,
prevents cancer, reduces radiation damage, antioxidativ, dissolves
stagnation.
Cooking time approx. 25 min
Calories p. portion: 96
4 portions
Allergens: L

Quantity of ingredients:
Water 2 cups / 450g. (yes)
Potato 4 pieces / 200g. (recommended)
Carrot 2 pieces / 100g. (recommended)
Celery root 1 piece / 500g. (recommended)
Pepper (ground) 1 pinch / 0,5g. (little)
Ground 1 pinch / 1g. (yes)
Garlic 1 clove / 3g. (recommended)
Salt 1 pinch / 1g. (little)
Lemon 1 teaspoon / 3g. (yes)
Basil (fresh) 1 Bunch / 50g. (recommended)
Peppers powder 1 pinch / 1g. (yes)
Sugar cane sugar 1 pinch / 1g. (little)
Olive oil 1 table spoon / 10g. (yes)

Cooking instructions:
Peeled and chopped 4 medium potatoes in a pot of hot water and 2 chopped medium carrots, a piece of celery root, a pinch of pepper, a pinch of ground cumin, crushed a small clove of garlic, a pinch of salt, 1 teaspoon of lemon juice, simmer until the Vegetables is soft.

Add 1 bunch finely chopped basil into one half of the soup and puree everything; stir in the other half of the basil; with rose paprika, a pinch of whole cane sugar, 1 tablespoon of olive oil or butter, freshly ground pepper, salt to taste.

9.59 Potatoes with curd cheese sauce

Improves digestion, supports urination, lowers cholesterol. Good to fight weakness, belching, diabetes, acute or chronic obstruction of the bowel, skin problems. Good to fight Bloating, cramping in gastrointestinal complaints.
Cooking time approx. 45 min
Calories p. portion: 414
6 portions
Allergens: G

Quantity of ingredients:
Potato 2,2 lbs / 1000g. (recommended)
Curd cheese 20% 1,1 lbs / 500g. (yes)
Cream, sweet 30% 5/8 oz / 200g. (little)
Edam cheese 3 oz / 80g. (little)
Dill 1 Bunch / 100g. (recommended)
Corn germ oil 1 teaspoon / 3g. (yes)
Pepper (ground) 1 pinch / 0,2g. (little)
Salt 1/2 teaspoon / 1g. (little)
Sunflower seeds 1/8 lbs - 2oz / 40g. (little)

Cooking instructions:
Wash the potatoes and cook in plenty of water for about 20 minutes.
Stir the creamy cheese with the cream and cottage cheese. Wash the
sprouts, finely chop. Stir in with the chopped dill. (For the baby, mix 150
g. of pot with the oil.) Mix the rest with pepper, salt and the sunflower
seeds. Peel the potatoes, arrange (for the baby 200 g.) with the pot.

9.60 Pumpkin curry

Promotes digestion and sweating, Dissolves stagnation, strengthens
lungs and spleen, diuretic, reduces blood glucose, forcing spleen and
digestive system, detoxifying, strengthens the muscles and bones.
Cooking time approx. 20 min
Calories p. portion: 193
3 portions
Allergens:

Quantity of ingredients:
Pumpkin 3/4 lbs / 300g. (recommended)
Olive oil 2 table spoons / 30g. (yes)
Coriander 1 pinch / 1g. (recommended)
Pepper (ground) 1 pinch / 0,5g. (little)
Curry 1 pinch / 1g. (little)
Water 1/4 cup / 50g. (yes)
Salt 1 pinch / 1g. (little)
Parsley 1 table spoon / 7g. (recommended)
Cardamom 1 pinch / 1g. (recommended)
Turmeric (yellow root) 1 pinch / 1g. (recommended)
Rice (whole grain) 1/2 cup / 60g. (yes)
Water 3 cups / 300g. (yes)
Salt 1 pinch / 1g. (little)

Cooking instructions:
Heat olive oil in pan. Steam the pumpkin cut in cubes, season with cilantro, pepper and curry, simmer with a little water, salt with sea salt, add chopped parsley with cardamom and turmeric, simmer on a small fire for about 10 minutes, depending on the pumpkin, the pumpkin should still be firm.

Place the rice in salted water, bring to the boil and let it simmer over low heat for about 15 minutes.

9.61 Pumpkin dumplings with tomato and parsley sauce

Protects the digestive system. Good to fight loss of appetite, flatulence, calms nerves and stomach, helps to digest fat, reduces blood pressure, stimulates liver function, dissolves stagnation.
Cooking time approx. 30 min
Calories p. portion: 380
2 portions
Allergens: ACG

Quantity of ingredients:
Hokkaido pumpkin 1/4 lbs - 4oz / 100g. (recommended)
Chicken egg 2 pieces / 120g. (little)
Wheat flour 1/2-1/3 cup / 120g. (yes)
Salt 1 pinch / 1g. (little)
Pepper (ground) 1 pinch / 0,5g. (little)
Nutmeg 1 pinch / 0,2g. (recommended)
Lemon peel 1/2 teaspoon / 2g. (yes)
Parmesan 2 table spoons / 20g. (little)
Onion (spring onion) 2 pieces / 40g. (little)
Tomato 1/4 lbs - 4oz / 100g. (recommended)
Parsley 1/2 bunch / 50g. (recommended)
Salt 1 pinch / 1g. (little)

Cooking instructions:
Peel the pumpkin with a sharp knife, remove the seeds and cut the pulp into large cubes. Wrap pumpkin in aluminum foil, bake in preheated oven at 200°C/392°F for 20 minutes. Pour off any spilled pumpkin juice. Finely crush the pumpkin with the fork. Stir pumpkin and egg until smooth. Stir in so much flour until a dough is formed, from which dumplings can be cut off. Season the mixture with lemon zest, salt, pepper and nutmeg.

Cut off small dumplings with a teaspoon. Leave pumpkin dumplings in boiling salted water for approx. 7 minutes.

Roast the onion in a frying pan until lightly fry the tomato cubes, salt and the chopped parsley.

Arrange pumpkin dumplings in portions with the tomato parsley sauce. Parmesan to hand.

9.62 Quinoa piquant with avocado

Anti-inflammatory, good to fight swelling, pain and itching. Reduces blood pressure, strengthens immune system. Strengthens gastrointestinal function, expands blood vessels. Good to fight gastrointestinal complaints.
Cooking time approx. 20 min
Calories p. portion: 561
2 portions
Allergens:

Quantity of ingredients:
Water 1 1/2 cups / 240g. (yes)
Quinoa 1 cup / 100g. (yes)
Carrot 1 piece shredded / 100g. (recommended)
Onion (spring onion) 2 table spoons (chopped) / 12g. (little)
Curcuma 1/2 teaspoon / 1g. (yes)
Avocado 1 piece soft / 300g. (recommended)
Salt 1 pinch / 0,5g. (little)
Pepper (ground) 1 pinch / 0,2g. (little)
Linseed oil 2 teaspoons / 4g. (yes)

Cooking instructions:
Put quinoa in hot water.
Add grated carrot, pepper and salt, finely chopped spring onion and turmeric.
Simmer about 20 minutes, pull from the fire.
Add pre-cut avocado.
Add a dash of oil and sprinkle with fresh parsley and gomasio.

Spices and herbs: turmeric, cardamom, cress, parsley, chives.
Variation: For those who want more hearty, you can also use a sardine from organic fish preserves. If you are the "protein type", this breakfast will hold on for a long time!

9.63 Quinoa with peach

Supports erythrocyte production, relieves fatigue, relaxes. Good to fight gastrointestinal complaints. Relieves pain, detoxifying, bactericide.
Cooking time approx. 20 min
Calories p. portion: 248
2 portions
Allergens:

Quantity of ingredients:
Quinoa 1 cup / 100g. (yes)
Water 1 1/2 cups / 240g. (yes)
Honey 2 teaspoons / 4g. (yes)
Peaches 2 pieces / 240g. (yes)
Linseed oil 2 teaspoons / 4g. (yes)
Lemon Balm (fresh) 1 teaspoon (chopped) / 1g. (recommended)
Cinnamon ground 1 pinch / 0,2g. (recommended)
Vanilla 1 pinch / 0,2g. (yes)

Cooking instructions:
In the evening: Put quinoa in hot water and boil soft, covered 15 to 20 minutes.
In the morning: Warm up quinoa with 1 tablespoon water.
Steam lightly Peaches in a saucepan or add them fresh. Decorate with fresh lemon balm.

Summer: nectarines, apricots
Winter: Pickled fruit, pear, apples

9.64 Radish with horseradish

Stimulates liver function, detoxifying. Promotes digestion, improves blood circulation, supports urination, reduces thirst.
Cooking time approx. 30 min
Calories p. portion: 196
2 portions
Allergens: GNO

Quantity of ingredients:
Butter organic 1 table spoon / 8g. (yes)
Radish (white, green, purple-red) 1/2 piece / 50g. (yes)
Water 2 table spoons / 10g. (yes)
Lemon juice 2 table spoons / 20g. (yes)
White wine 2 table spoons / 20g. (little)

Pepper powder (hot) 1 pinch / 0,2g. (yes)
Sesame oil 1 teaspoon / 3g. (yes)
Radish horseradish 2 table spoons / 20g. (recommended)
Salt 1 pinch / 0,5g. (little)
Parsley 1 Bunch (chopped) / 80g. (recommended)
Rice long grain rice 1/2 cup / 60g. (yes)
Water 3 cups / 300g. (yes)
Salt 1 pinch / 0,5g. (little)

Cooking instructions:
In a hot pan melt the butter, sautéed into stripes cut radish. Add cold water, lemon juice, white wine, a pinch of rose paprika and stir in the sesame oil; with 2 - 3 tablespoons fresh grated horseradish (alternatively 1 teaspoon from the glass), salt to taste; Sprinkle with chopped parsley.

Place the rice with the water, salt and cook for about 15 minutes.

9.65 Refreshing cucumber soup with potatoes

Diuretic, detoxifying, suppresses conversion of sugar into fat, lowers cholesterol, prevents cancer, reduces inflammation, improves digestion, lowers cholesterol, dissolves stagnation, improves blood circulation, stimulates appetite.
Cooking time approx. 15 min
Calories p. portion: 148
3 portions
Allergens: GN

Quantity of ingredients:
Sesame oil 1 table spoon / 10g. (yes)
Potato 4 pieces / 300g. (recommended)
Onion (spring onion) 3 pieces / 60g. (little)
Pepper (ground) 1 pinch / 0,5g. (little)
Nutmeg 1 pinch / 1g. (recommended)
Salt 1 pinch / 1g. (little)
Lemon 1/2 piece / 25g. (yes)
Cucumber 2 pieces / 500g. (recommended)
Cream, sweet 30% 1 table spoon / 10g. (little)
Dill 1 table spoon / 15g. (recommended)

Cooking instructions:
Sauté sesame oil, chopped potatoes, plenty of spring onions in a hot pot; add pepper, a little nutmeg, salt, lemon juice, hot water, diced cucumber; simmer for about 10 minutes and then puree; add some sweet cream as you like, fresh dill.

Variation: Add a little chili, oregano, thyme or rosemary to soften the cooling effect.

9.66 Rice congee with honey pear and black sesame

Promotes digestion, supports urination, good to fight blood circulation disorders, thromboses, risk of embolism, high blood pressure, a headache, heart attack and stroke.
Cooking time approx. 10 min - 3 hours
Calories p. portion: 158
2 portions
Allergens: N

Quantity of ingredients:
Basic recipe for a rice soup (Congee) 1 1/2 cups / 240g. (recommended)
Pear 2 pieces / 300g. (recommended)
Sesame, black 1 teaspoon / 3g. (recommended)

Cooking instructions:
Cook rice congee according to basic recipe.
Fill pot with 3 cm of water and heat till it boils. Quarter the pears (with the skin and seeds) and simmer them covered with black sesame for 10 minutes. Mix with the rice.

9.67 Rice noodle soup with shiitake mushrooms

Very light and powerful. Strengthens the immune system.
Cooking time approx. 20 min
Calories p. portion: 66
2 portions
Allergens: L

Quantity of ingredients:
Rice noodles 2 handful / 20g. (yes)
Shiitake, dried 4-6 pieces / 5g. (yes)
Basic recipe for a vegetable soup 1 1/2 cups / 240g. (recommended)
Chinese cabbage 1 cup / 60g. (recommended)
Lovage 1 teaspoon / 3g. (recommended)
Miso 2 table spoons / 18g. (yes)

Cooking instructions:
Soak rice noodles and shiitake mushrooms separately in cold water.
Heat the vegetable broth and add the soaked shiitake mushrooms cut
into strips and simmer gently. Cut Chinese cabbage into noodles, add
lovage green and rice noodles and let it steep for a while. Before
serving, stir in Miso dissolved in a little cooled water. Recommendation:
Suitable at the beginning of each meal, also for breakfast

9.68 Rice with parsnips

Rich in vitamins, minerals potassium and zinc. Good to fight blood
circulation disorders, thrombose, risk of embolism, high blood pressure,
a headache, heart attack and stroke, yeast infections.
Cooking time approx. 45 min
Calories p. portion: 206
3 portions
Allergens:

Quantity of ingredients:
Rice variety any 1 cup / 120g. (yes)
Water 1 1/2 cups / 200g. (yes)
Salt 1 pinch / 1g. (little)
Parsnip 3-4 pieces / 450g. (recommended)
Olive oil 1 table spoon / 10g. (yes)
Sage 1 teaspoon / 3g. (yes)

Cooking instructions:
Peel the parsnips and cut into slices. Fry for a short time in oil. Add the
rice and fry again for a short time. Add the water and cook it at least 30
min. Sprinkle with fresh chopped sage.

9.69 Rice with stewed vegetables

Reduces blood pressure, strengthens immune system, prevents cancer, reduces radiation damage, extremely low fat content, good to fight blood circulation disorders, thrombose, risk of embolism, a headache, heart attack and stroke. Is diuretic.
Cooking time approx. 20 min
Calories p. portion: 166
2 portions
Allergens: L

Quantity of ingredients:
Rice variety any 1/2 cup / 60g. (yes)
Water 3 cups / 300g. (yes)
Lemon peel 1 piece / 3g. (yes)
Water 1/2 cup / 0g. (yes)
Carrot 2 pieces / 180g. (recommended)
Celery sticks 1/2 piece / 5g. (recommended)
Champignon 1/2 cup / 50g. (yes)
Cress 2 table spoons / 20g. (yes)
Linseed oil 1 dash / 3g. (yes)

Cooking instructions:
Cook rice according to basic recipe with a piece of lemon peel.
Steam chopped carrots, celery and mushrooms until soft.
Then sprinkle with cress. Then add a dash of high quality cold oil.

9.70 Roasted barley patties

Improves digestion, lowers cholesterol, good to fight diarrhea, ulceration, joint pain, stomach problems. Promotes spleen and liver, reduces blood pressure, strengthens immune system, prevents cancer, reduces radiation damage, stimulates liver function.
Cooking time approx. 1 1/2 hours
Calories p. portion: 398
3 portions
Allergens: ACN

Quantity of ingredients:
Water 1 1/2 cups / 250g. (yes)
Barley grouts 1 cup / 120g. (yes)
Potato 1 piece / 140g. (recommended)
Carrot 1 piece / 120g. (recommended)
Champignon 2-3 pieces / 25g. (yes)

Chicken egg 1 piece / 55g. (little)
Onion white 1 piece / 50g. (little)
Ginger fresh 1/2 teaspoon / 1g. (recommended)
Pepper (ground) 1 pinch / 0,5g. (little)
Salt 1 pinch / 1g. (little)
Lemon 1/2 piece / 15g. (yes)
Parsley 2 table spoons / 15g. (recommended)
Peppers powder 1 pinch / 1g. (yes)
Sesame oil 2 table spoons / 50g. (yes)
Bread roll 1 piece / 35g. (yes)

Cooking instructions:
Preparation:
Place 2 large cups of hot water in a saucepan; add 1 large cup of barley porridge; simmer for 2 minutes while stirring; then let it swell for 20 minutes on the switched off stove; take down and let cool.

Cook in boiling water 1 large potato, chopped and cut.

Soak 1 roll in hot water and squeeze well.
Then: Mix the barley groats and crushed the potato. Add 1 grated carrot, 2 - 3 chopped mushrooms, 1 egg, 1 finely chopped onion, 1/2 teaspoon grated ginger, a pinch of pepper, a pinch of salt, a little lemon juice, chopped parsley, plenty of rose paprika; knead well and form patties; heat sesame oil in a hot pan; fry the patties for about 15 minutes over a gentle heat; turn at half time.
Also fits well: lettuce, soybean vegetables.

9.71 Rosemary Potatoes

Reduces Inflammation, improves digestion, regenerates skin, supports urination, lowers cholesterol. Rosemary stimulates digestion, strengthens lung, promotes spleen and kidney, dries out.
Cooking time approx. 30 min
Calories p. portion: 188
2 portions
Allergens:

Quantity of ingredients:
Potato 6-8 pieces / 420g. (recommended)
Salt (herbal) 1 pinch / 1g. (little)
Olive oil 1 table spoon / 10g. (yes)
Rosemary 1 teaspoon / 2g. (yes)

Cooking instructions:
Cut the potatoes into half´s, apply a little olive oil on the cut surface, then salt, sprinkle 2 - 3 rosemary needles on the potatoes.
Place the potatoes on the baking tray and bake them in the preheated oven for approx. 25 minutes to 190°C/374°F.

9.72 Salmon on tomato-spinach

Promotes bowel movement, improves blood circulation, forcing spleen and bowel, strengthens blood, reduces inflammation, improves digestion, regenerates skin, supports urination, lowers cholesterol, promotes sweating, dissolves stagnation.
Cooking time approx. 1 hour
Calories p. portion: 365
6 portions
Allergens: D

Quantity of ingredients:
Potato 1,1 lbs / 500g. (recommended)
Salt 1 pinch / 1g. (little)
Salmon 1,3 lbs / 600g. (yes)
Rapeseed oil 2 teaspoons / 24g. (yes)
Tomato 1/4 lbs - 4oz / 100g. (recommended)
Spinach 1,5 lbs / 700g. (recommended)
Salt 1 pinch / 1g. (little)
Pine nuts 4 table spoons / 40g. (little)
Leek 1/4 lbs - 4oz / 120g. (little)
Olive oil 4 table spoons / 40g. (yes)
Salt 1 pinch / 1g. (little)
Pepper white (ground) 1 pinch / 0,5g. (little)

Cooking instructions:
Peel the potato and cut into cubes, cook in salted water.
Cut the salmon into portions and fry slowly and evenly in a frying pan from both sides, seasoned with salt and pepper, then add the pine nuts and lightly roast. Blanch spinach in salted water.
Lightly sweat the finely chopped leek with a little rapeseed oil, add the blanched spinach and heat evenly.
Just before serving, add the halved cocktail tomatoes to the spinach and season the vegetables well with salt and pepper.
Arrange the spinach and leek tomato bed with the potatoes, add the salmon and sprinkle with the salted pine nuts.
Drizzle with a little olive oil and serve the dish.

9.73 Semolina dumpling & mascarpone and strawberry sauce

Relieves pain and inflammation, little laxative. Protects the digestive system. Detoxifying, affects anorexia, good to fight flatulence, inflammatory bowel disease, obesity, gout, stomach ulcers, stomach cramps, rheumatism, heartburn, twelffinger intestinal ulcers.
Cooking time approx. 25 min
Calories p. portion: 331
3 portions
Allergens: AG

Quantity of ingredients:
Cow's milk (1.5% fat) 1 1/2 cups / 400g. (yes)
Wheat semolina 0,2 lbs / 70g. (yes)
Cinnamon ground 1 pinch / 0,5g. (recommended)
Lemon peel 1 pinch / 1g. (yes)
Honey 1 teaspoon / 3g. (yes)
Vanilla pod 1 pinch / 0,5g. (recommended)
Mascarpone cheese 3 oz / 80g. (yes)
Strawberries 1,1 lbs / 500g. (yes)
Honey 1 table spoon / 10g. (yes)

Cooking instructions:
In a small saucepan, heat the milk till it boil while stirring. Stir in semolina, cinnamon and lemon peel and cook 6 minutes stirring until thick, firm paste.

Mix the semolina, honey, vanilla and mascarpone into a smooth mixture with the hand mixer. Allow the mass to cool in the refrigerator.

For the sauce, puree strawberries with honey in a blender.
Spread a few spoons of fruit sauce on a large plate. With 2 tablespoons, cut off dumplings from the semolina mass (to prevent sticking, rinse in cold water again and again). Put the dumplings on the fruit souce.
It looks especially nice when the dessert is still garnished with a few berries and herbal leaves.

9.74 Semolina porridge with banana

Regulates gastrointestinal function, reduces inflammation, antiallergic, good to fight blood circulation disorders.
Cooking time approx. 15 min
Calories p. portion: 307
1 portions
Allergens: AG

Quantity of ingredients:
Cow's milk (whole milk 3.5% fat) 3/4 cup - 6 oz / 200g. (yes)
Spelled semolina 2 table spoons / 30g. (yes)
Butter organic 1 teaspoon / 4g. (yes)
Banana 1/2 piece / 50g. (recommended)

Cooking instructions:
Heat the half of the milk in a small pot. Add the semolina and boil it shortly in the milk. Let it swell at low heat for 3 minutes with constant stirring. Remove the pot from the heat, add the remaining milk with the snow bean and place the mush in a small bowl. Add the butter and the battered banana.
For adults, a pinch of cinnamon can be spread over it.

9.75 Sliced chicken with walnuts and sherry

Strengthens blood, strengthens bone marrow, strengthens gastrointestinal function, expands blood vessels, prevents cancer, promotes perspiration, reduces blood lipids, stimulates.
Cooking time approx. 25 min
Calories p. portion: 304
4 portions
Allergens: EGHN

Quantity of ingredients:
Butter organic 2 table spoons / 35g. (yes)
Walnuts 2 table spoons / 25g. (little)
Ginger fresh 1/2 teaspoon / 2g. (recommended)
Onion (shallot) 2 pieces / 40g. (little)
Salt 1 pinch / 1g. (little)
Chicken meat 3/4 lbs / 300g. (yes)
Peppers powder 1 pinch / 1g. (yes)
Sesame, white 1 teaspoon / 2g. (yes)
Black fungus mushroom 4 pieces / 3g. (yes)
Shiitake, dried 4 pieces / 5g. (yes)

Soy sauce 1 dash / 3g. (yes)
Rice (whole grain) 1 cup / 120g. (yes)
Water 6 cups / 550g. (yes)
Salt 1 pinch / 1g. (little)

Cooking instructions:
Heat butter or sesame oil in a hot pan; Sauté walnuts, copious grated ginger, chopped shallots or onions; Add the salt and the sliced chicken and sauté everything; Rose paprika, roasted sesame, soaked black fungus, shiitake mushrooms or mushrooms; with a shot sherry; infuse with water; Simmer for 5 to 10 minutes until the meat is cooked; Season with soy sauce.

Place the rice in salted water, heat till it boils and let it simmer over low heat for about 15 minutes.

This fits: lamb's lettuce, Radicchio

9.76 Sliced turkey with zucchini

Improves digestion, regenerates skin, supports urination, lowers cholesterol, diuretic. Strengthens blood, strengthens bone marrow. promotes spleen and liver, reduces blood pressure, strengthens immune system.
Cooking time approx. 1 hour
Calories p. portion: 282
6 portions
Allergens: AEGL

Quantity of ingredients:
Turkey breast meat 3/4 lbs / 300g. (yes)
Lemon juice 1 table spoon / 10g. (yes)
Basil 1 teaspoon / 2g. (recommended)
Zucchini 1,8 lbs / 800g. (recommended)
Corn germ oil 2 table spoons / 20g. (yes)
Basic recipe for a vegetable soup 1/4 lbs - 4oz / 125g. (recommended)
Cream, sweet 30% 1/4 lbs - 4oz / 125g. (little)
Soy sauce 1 table spoon / 10g. (yes)
Oat fusion (baby food) 2 table spoons / 16g. (yes)
Potato 1,8 lbs / 800g. (recommended)

Cooking instructions:
Cut the turkey meat into thin strips, drizzle with the lemon juice and sprinkle with the basil. Wash and peel the zucchini, removing the stems and flowers. Grate the zucchini coarsely.

Heat 1 tablespoon of oil and fry the turkey meat. Add the vegetable stock and add the cream, put on the lid and simmer for about 10 minutes on low heat. Add the zucchini rasp and the melted flakes. Put the lid back on and steam again for about 10 minutes.

For the baby: Crush about 70 g of potatoes. Put about 150 g of zucchini with meat over it. Chop the meat, mix with the remaining oil.

For the family: Add the sliced meat with the broth, add the soy sauce and cook for another 1-2 minutes. Serve with the potatoes.

9.77 Spelled-grid porridge with berries of the season

Little laxative, strengthens immune system, activated cell metabolism, reduces inflammation. Has a stabilizing effect on the blood circulation, good to fight blood circulation disorders.
Cooking time approx. 15 min
Calories p. portion: 244
2 portions
Allergens: AGH

Quantity of ingredients:
Cow's milk (1.5% fat) 1/2 cup / 125g. (yes)
Water 1/2 cup / 125g. (yes)
Spelled semolina 5 table spoons / 50g. (yes)
Butter organic 2 teaspoons / 20g. (yes)
Berries of the season 1/4 lbs - 4oz / 100g. (recommended)
Honey 1-2 teaspoons / 5g. (yes)
Almond 1-2 teaspoons / 5g. (yes)
Peppermint 3-4 leaves / 2g. (yes)
Cinnamon ground 1 pinch / 0,5g. (recommended)
Vanilla 1 pinch / 0,2g. (yes)
Cocoa 1 pinch / 0,5g. (yes)
Coconut grated 1 table spoon / 10g. (yes)

Cooking instructions:
Stir in spelled semolina in cold water and boil slowly over medium heat. After boiling, remove from the heat and let simmer for a few minutes. Depending on the desired consistency, some water may have to be added. Stir in the butter and fine grated nuts in the mash and raspberries. Serve with honey or whole-grain sugar as desired.
Spices and aromas: fresh mint, cinnamon or vanilla, cocoa, coconut

Summer: raspberries, blueberries, strawberries

9.78 Strawberry bananas mash

Regulates gastrointestinal function. Promotes digestion.
Cooking time approx. 10 min
Calories p. portion: 30
10 portions
Allergens:
Quantity of ingredients:
Banana 1 piece / 200g. (recommended)
Strawberries 5/8 oz / 200g. (yes)
Orange 1/2 piece / 70g. (yes)

Cooking instructions:
Peel the banana. Wash the strawberries, pluck from the stems. Put both in a mixing bowl. Add the orange juice and finely grate everything. Put the marrow in an ice cube maker and freeze. Transfer the frozen cubes to a cool box (shelf life of up to 2 months). Small portions are ideal for mixing with yogurt or cottage cheese.

9.79 Supplementary nutrition

Protein-rich drink with very high energy density. Optimized protein content balances nitrogen losses and promotes protein anabolism.
Cooking time approx. 5 min
Calories p. portion: 1045
1 portions
Allergens:

Quantity of ingredients:
Supplementary nutrition 1 package / 250g. (yes)

Cooking instructions:
Use only as directed by the physician or therapist.

9.80 Sweet potato pancakes with basil pesto

Strengthens the immune system, reduces fat, Improves digestion, calms nerves and stomach, dissolves stones, improves blood circulation, strengthens the muscles, antioxidativ.
Cooking time approx. 30 min
Calories p. portion: 625
3 portions
Allergens: ACH

Quantity of ingredients:
Sweet potato 4 pieces / 500g. (recommended)
Onion read 1/2 piece / 30g. (little)
Basil 1 table spoon / 10g. (recommended)
Chicken egg 2 pieces / 140g. (little)
Spelled wholemeal flour 3 oz / 80g. (yes)
Salt 1 pinch / 0,5g. (little)
Olive oil 1/4 cup / 20g. (yes)
Salt 1 teaspoon (coarse) / 3g. (little)
Basil Handful / 15g. (recommended)
Parsley Handful / 15g. (recommended)
Garlic 2 cloves / 3g. (recommended)
Walnuts 1/8 lbs - 2oz / 60g. (little)
Olive oil 2 table spoons / 20g. (yes)

Cooking instructions:
Sweet Potato Buffer: Wash the sweet potato thoroughly, but do not peel, and grate into a large bowl. Add onion, basil, egg and flour, mix well and sprinkle with salt. The mixture can be formed into buffers. Bake in a preheated tube on a baking tray coated with oil for 4 to 5 minutes on both sides.

Basil Pesto: Add the salt, chopped basil and parsley and crushed garlic in a small bowl and crush (if available, use the mortar). Add the grated walnuts. While stirring, add enough olive oil until the desired consistency is achieved.

9.81 Tea from anise

Anise (wild fennel) promotes digestion, forcing spleen and stomach.
Cooking time approx. 15 min
Calories p. portion: 3
4 portions
Allergens:

Quantity of ingredients:
Anise (Common Fennel) 1 teaspoon / 3g. (recommended)
Water 2 cup / 500g. (yes)

Cooking instructions:
Heat the water till it boils and put it aside. Add anise.
10 min. to let go.
Pour through a tea strainer. Sweet to taste with honey.

In order to achieve a salutary effect, you should drink 2 cups of anise tea per day.

9.82 Tea from fennel

Harmonizes stomach, less bloating.
Cooking time approx. 10 min
Calories p. portion: 0
4 portions
Allergens:

Quantity of ingredients:
Fennel tea 2 table spoons / 20g. (recommended)
Water 2 cup / 500g. (yes)

Cooking instructions:
Heat the water till it boils and put it aside. Add fennel tea and 10 min. to let go. Sweet to taste with honey. Strain when pouring.

9.83 Tea from ginger with honey

Honey relieves pain, detoxifying, bactericide.
Fresh ginger encourages digestion, detoxifying, strengthens bodily production, promotes perspiration, reduces blood lipids, stimulates, dissolves stagnation.
Cooking time approx. 30 min
Calories p. portion: 5
4 portions
Allergens:

Quantity of ingredients:
Ginger fresh 1 teaspoon / 3g. (recommended)
Water 2 cup / 500g. (yes)
Honey 2 teaspoons / 6g. (yes)

Cooking instructions:
Heat the water till it boils and put it aside. Add ginger and 20-30 min. to let go. Sweet to taste with honey.

9.84 Tea from yarrow

Blood detoxifying, blood stilling, cramp-dissolving, improves digestion, good to fight flatulence, diabetes, diarrhea, constipation, bleeding.
Cooking time approx. 15 min
Calories p. portion: 0
2 portions
Allergens:

Quantity of ingredients:
Yarrow tea 2-4 teaspoons / 6g. (recommended)
Water 2 cup / 500g. (yes)

Cooking instructions:
Heat the water till it boils and put it aside. Add yarrow and 10 min. to let go. Strain. Sweet to taste with honey.

9.85 Tea Green tea

Green tea promotes digestion, supports urination, dissolves mucus, detoxifying, stimulates nerves, reduces blood lipids, lowers cholesterol, reduces inflammation.
Cooking time approx. 10 min
Calories p. portion: 2
1 portions
Allergens:

Quantity of ingredients:
Green tea 1 teaspoon / 2g. (recommended)
Water 1 cup / 120g. (yes)

Cooking instructions:
For each cup you use a teaspoonful or a teabag.
Pour green tea only with 60 to 80 ° C / 140 to 176 °F hot water, otherwise it will be bitter.
If the tea has a stimulating effect, let it draw for two to three minutes. It has a calming effect for a duration of five minutes (no longer, otherwise it will be bitter!).
Another method: Pour the tea leaves with about 70 ° C / 158 °F hot water and pour the water immediately again. Then just pour hot water again. The bitter substances disappear and the tea gets a milder aroma.

9.86 Tea mixture against intestinal inertia

Promote digestion, Strengthens the stomach, Diuretic and generally powerful, good to fight loss of appetite, improves digestion and stomach ailments.
Cooking time approx. 20 min
Calories p. portion: 1
8 portions
Allergens:

Quantity of ingredients:
Gentian root 1 table spoon / 20g. (recommended)
Kalmus 1 table spoon / 20g. (yes)
Blackthorn (Sloe) 1 table spoon / 20g. (yes)
Water 4 cup / 1000g. (yes)

Cooking instructions:
Preparation:
Mix gentian 20 g kalmus 20 g and blackthorn 20 g.

Preparation: 1 tablespoon of the mixture to 1 cup as an infusion, let stand for 15-20 minutes. Use: Drink 1 cup warm in the morning and evening.

9.87 Tea mixture appetizing

Ginger powder is warming, promotes sweating, dissolves stagnation.
Cooking time approx. 10 min
Calories p. portion: 0
4 portions
Allergens:

Quantity of ingredients:
Bitter orange peel 1 teaspoons / 3g. (yes)
Yarrow tea 1 teaspoons / 3g. (recommended)
Ginger powder 1g. Or 0,034oz / 1g. (recommended)
Horehound leaves 1 teaspoons / 3g. (yes)
Water 2 cups / 500g. (yes)

Cooking instructions:
Brew one tablespoon of tea mixture with half a liter of water and leave for 10 min. to let go. Then strain and drink in small sips before eating.

9.88 Tomato soup

Promotes digestion, helps to digest fat, supports urination, reduces blood pressure, dissolves stagnation. Contains unsaturated fatty acids, is antioxidativ.
Cooking time approx. 10 min
Calories p. portion: 100
2 portions
Allergens:

Quantity of ingredients:
Olive oil 1 table spoon / 15g. (yes)
Onion white 1 piece / 60g. (little)
Cinnamon ground 1 pinch / 1g. (recommended)
Basil (fresh) 1 teaspoon / 2g. (recommended)
Pepper (ground) 1 pinch / 0,5g. (little)
Salt 1 pinch / 1g. (little)
Tomato 6 pieces / 250g. (recommended)
Peppers powder 1 pinch / 1g. (yes)
Water 5/8 lbs - 8oz / 250g. (yes)

Cooking instructions:
Roast the onion in a pot. Salt and spices. Briefly roast. Put washed and quartered tomatoes in the pan. Stir and sauté briefly. Add a quart of water and heat till it boils. Cook for a quarter of an hour and puree.

9.89 Tomato with mozzarella

Promotes digestion, helps to digest fat, supports urination, reduces blood pressure. Affects anorexia, good to fight flatulence, inflammatory bowel disease, bloating and nausea. Relaxing and reassuring.
Cooking time approx. 5 min
Calories p. portion: 436
1 portions
Allergens: AG

Quantity of ingredients:
Mozzarella 1 piece / 50g. (yes)
Tomato 2 pieces / 100g. (recommended)
Salt 1 pinch / 1g. (little)
Basil (fresh) 5 leaves / 6g. (recommended)
Olive oil 2 table spoons / 20g. (yes)
White bread (wheat bread) 2 slices / 40g. (little)

Cooking instructions:
Cut tomatoes and mozzarella into slices. Serve with salt, basil and olive oil. Serve with white bread.

9.90 Vegetable bowl with Provencal pistou

Promotes spleen and liver, reduces blood pressure, strengthens immune system, prevents cancer, reduces radiation damage, forcing spleen, dissolves stagnation. Relieves constipation, strengthens mother milk production.
Cooking time approx. 1 1/2 hours
Calories p. portion: 138
8 portions
Allergens: AGL

Quantity of ingredients:
Tomato 5/8 oz / 200g. (recommended)
Olive oil 2 table spoons / 30g. (yes)
Garlic 1 clove / 5g. (recommended)
Toast bread (whole grain) 1 slice / 5g. (yes)
Parmesan 1 oz / 30g. (little)
Basil (fresh) 1 Bunch / 125g. (recommended)
Salt 1 pinch / 2g. (little)
Pepper (ground) 1 pinch / 1g. (little)
Oregano dried 1 teaspoon / 3g. (recommended)
Basic recipe for a vegetable soup 3 lbs / 1250g. (recommended)
Carrot 3/8 lbs - 6oz / 150g. (recommended)
Celery root 1/4 lbs - 4oz / 100g. (recommended)
Broccoli 5/8 oz / 200g. (recommended)
Fennel 1 piece / 250g. (recommended)
Thyme dried 1/2 teaspoon / 2g. (yes)
Oregano dried 1/2 teaspoon / 2g. (recommended)
Bay leaf 1 piece / 0,5g. (recommended)
Peas, green 1/8 lbs - 2oz / 50g. (recommended)
Onion (spring onion) 4 pieces / 80g. (little)
Potato 1/4 lbs - 4oz / 100g. (recommended)

Cooking instructions:
Sauce:
Tear off tomatoes and cut into small pieces. Reduce in a pot with a little olive oil, finely chopped garlic. Add 1 slice of dry toasted bread (crumbed), fresh finely grated Parmesan, finely chopped basil, oregano, salt and pepper.

Soup:
Boil the vegetable broth according to the basic recipe, add coarsely sliced carrots, diced celery, diced potatoes, small florets, broccoli, finely

chopped fennel tuber, peas, thyme, oregano and the bay leaf. let cook 10 minutes.

Cut 4 scallions into thin rings, add them and cook another 2 min.

Pour sauce into a soup bowl. First only a few tablespoons. Stir boiling broth with it, then stir in the soup little by little.

9.91 Vitamin drink

Regulates gastrointestinal function, promotes spleen and liver, reduces blood pressure, strengthens immune system, prevents cancer, reduces radiation damage, supports urination, quenches thirst, calms the stomach, prevents cancer.
Cooking time approx. 5 min
Calories p. portion: 172
3 portions
Allergens:

Quantity of ingredients:
Orange juice 1 cup / 300g. (recommended)
Carrot 5/8 oz / 200g. (recommended)
Banana 2 pieces / 300g. (recommended)
Kiwi 1 piece / 20g. (yes)

Cooking instructions:
Chop oranges, carrots, bananas and kiwi and finely puree with the blender.

9.92 Warming carrot soup

Strengthens and warms, reduces blood pressure, strengthens immune system, prevents cancer, reduces radiation damage, strengthens gastrointestinal function.
Cooking time approx. 30 min
Calories p. portion: 133
3 portions
Allergens: HL

Quantity of ingredients:
Carrot 4 pieces / 250g. (recommended)
Walnut oil 2 table spoons / 20g. (yes)
Onion (shallot) 2 pieces / 40g. (little)
Anise (Common Fennel) 1/2 teaspoon / 1g. (recommended)

Nutmeg 1 pinch / 1g. (recommended)
Ginger fresh 1/2 teaspoon / 1g. (recommended)
Salt 1 pinch / 1g. (little)
Basic recipe for a vegetable soup 2 cup / 500g. (recommended)
Parsley 1 table spoon / 10g. (recommended)

Cooking instructions:
Heat walnut oil in a hot pot and fry onions; steam the carrots in it; add anise, nutmeg, a little ginger, salt and sauté everything; add water or vegetable- or meat stock; cook everything soft and then puree; fold in parsley at the end.

Recommendation: Suitable for the cold season, especially if you use meat broth as a liquid for infusion.

9.93 Wheat fresh grain porridge with pears.

Promotes digestion, supports urination. Affects anorexia, good to fight flatulence, inflammatory bowel disease. Lowers cholesterol, is antiparasitic.
Cooking time approx. 25 min
Calories p. portion: 309
2 portions
Allergens: ANO

Quantity of ingredients:
Wheat 1 cup / 100g. (yes)
Water 2-4 cups / 350g. (yes)
Pear 2 pieces / 300g. (recommended)
Raisins 1 table spoon / 10g. (yes)
Sesame, white 1 table spoon / 8g. (yes)
Sunflower seeds 1 table spoon / 8g. (little)
Cardamom 1 pinch / 0,3g. (recommended)
Salt 1 pinch / 0,3g. (little)

Cooking instructions:
Preparation the night before: Wheat roughly cut; soak overnight.

In the morning: Put the wheat meal with a little hot water; simmer with stirring for about 15 minutes.
Meanwhile, add pear compote, raisins, crushed sesame, sunflower seeds, some ground cardamom, a small pinch of salt.
Variants: with grated apple or seasonal fruit.

9.94 Yellow lentil soup

Strengthens heart and kidney, diuretic, promotes spleen, calms the stomach, promotes digestion, strengthens immune system, prevents cancer, reduces radiation damage, stimulates liver function, antioxidativ.
Cooking time approx. 20 min
Calories p. portion: 155
7 portions
Allergens: A

Quantity of ingredients:
Lentils yellow 1 lbs / 500g. (yes)
Carrot 2 pieces / 150g. (recommended)
Kohlrabi 1 piece / 300g. (recommended)
Onion white 1 piece / 50g. (little)
Parsley 1/2 bunch / 100g. (recommended)
Turmeric (yellow root) 1 pinch / 1g. (recommended)
Cardamom 1 pinch / 1g. (recommended)
Salt 1 pinch / 1g. (little)
Olive oil 1 table spoon / 10g. (yes)
Water 4 cup / 1000g. (yes)
Lemon juice 1/2 piece / 15g. (yes)
White bread (wheat bread) 7 slices / 140g. (little)

Cooking instructions:
Wash lenses well in a colander. Heat oil in a pot. Add finely chopped onion, sliced carrots, diced kohlrabi and spices, sauté and salt. Add the lentils and cover with water and simmer for 20 minutes. Add water as needed and season with salt. Sprinkle with fresh parsley or fresh green cilantro and drizzle with lemon juice.
Here you can also use red lenses. (same cooking time).
Serve with white bread.

10 Effects of food

10.1 Use ingredients: recommendable

Acai powder
Acerola fruit nectar or powder
Anise (Common Fennel)
Apple (sour)
Apple (sweet)
Apple juice (natural cloudy)
Apple puree
Apricot
Apricot nectar
Apricots juice
Artichoke
Asparagus (green or white)
Aubergine
Avocado
Banana
Banana (cooking banana)
Basic recipe for a rice soup (Congee)
Basic recipe for a vegetable soup
(nutritious)
Basil
Basil (fresh)
Bay leaf
Berries of the season
Berry juice
Bitter Herb liqueur
Blueberry juice
Broccoli
Brussels sprouts
Cardamom
Carrot
Carrot (Early Carrot)
Carrot juice without sugar
Celery root
Celery sticks
Chard
Cherry juice
Chinese cabbage
Cinnamon ground
Cinnamon sticks
Compote (fruits of the season)
Coriander
Coriander (fresh)
Cranberries
Cream 10% coffee cream
Cucumber
Cumin (Caraway seed)
Currant jam (black)
Currant juice (black)
Dill

Fennel
Fennel seeds ground
Fennel tea
Fish pieces mixed (fresh water)
Fox nut, gorgon nut, makhana
Fruit mix juice
Garlic
Gentian root
Ginger fresh
Ginger powder
Gourd
Grape juice red
Grape juice white
Green tea
Ground caraway
Hibiscus
Hokkaido pumpkin
Kohlrabi
Kudzu
Lemon Balm (dried)
Lemon Balm (fresh)
Lily bulbs
Lovage
Mango juice
Manioc flour
Maple syrup
Mediterranean fish (cod, plaice,
haddock, sea eel, mackerel)
Nettles
Nutmeg
Okra
Orange juice
Oregano dried
Oregano fresh
Parsley
Parsley root
Parsnip
Pear
Pear juice
Peas, green
Peppermint tea
Peppers
Potato
Potato (mealy)
Pumpkin
Radish black
Radish horseradish
Rose hip tea
Salsify

Savory
Sesame, black
Spinach
Sweet potato
Tomato
Tomato juice
Tomato paste
Tomato puree
Topinambur
Turmeric (yellow root)
Turnips

Vanilla pod
Vegetable juice
Wax gourd
Wheat bran
Wheat flour whole grain
Wheat/Rye/Gray-black bread with yeast
Whole grain bread
Wholemeal flour
Yarrow
Yarrow tea
Zucchini

10.2 Use ingredients: yes

Adzuki beans
Agar agar (kelp)
Agave nectar
Agrimony
Almond
Almond marzipan
Aloe juice
Amaranth
Amaranth Pops
Anchovy / Sardine
Angelica root
Apricot dried
Apricot jam
Apricots
Arrowroot
Baking powder
Balm
Bamboo shoots
Banchatee (green tea)
barberry
Barley
Barley flour
Barley grass powder
Barley grouts
Barley malt
Barley not peeled
Basic recipe for a chicken soup
(warming)
Basic recipe for a fish soup
Batavia
Bean oil
Bearberry leaf
Beer (alcohol-free)
Beer (alcohol-reduced)
Bitter Lemon
Bitter orange peel
Black caraway
Black fungus mushroom
Blackberry dried (unripe fruit)
Blackberry jam

Blackberry leaves
Blackberry's
Black-eyed peas
Blackthorn (Sloe)
Blue mallow tee
Blueberry
Blueberry dried
Blueberry jam
Bocksdorn fruits (Fructus Lycii, Goji,
goji berry dried
Boletus mushroom
Borage
Borage oil
Boxhorn clover seeds

Bread roll
Bread with carob kernel flour
Breadcrumbs (wheat bread, bread roll)
Brie cheese
Buckbean
Buckwheat
Buckwheat (roasted) Kasha
Buckwheat whole grain
Bulgur (cereals)
Burdock root tea
Butter (half fat)
Butter beans white
Butter organic
Buttermilk
Calamari
Camembert
Cantaloupe
Capers in olive oil
Carambola (Star fruit)
Carob flour, St. john's bread
Carp
Cashews
Caviar
Cereal coffee
Chamomile

Chamomile tea
Champignon
Channa-Dal
Chanterelle
Chenpi (chinese tangerine bowl)
Cherry
Cherry (sour)
Cherry compote
Chervil
Chervil dried
Chestnut puree
Chestnuts
Chicken meat
Chickweed
Chicory
Chinese pearl barley
Chives
Chlorella (fresh water)
Chrysanthemum blossom tea
Clementine
Clementines
Clove
Cocoa
Coconut grated
Coconut meat
Cod
Codfish
Coffee
Coix (seeds) YiYi Ren
Cola drink
Corn
Corn (fast polenta)
Corn (roasted)
Corn flour
Corn germ oil
Corn Grease (Polenta)
Corn silk tea
Corn starch
Cottage cheese
Couscous
Cow's milk (1.5% fat)
Cow's milk (whole milk 3.5% fat)
Crab
Cranberry
Cranberry
Cranberry jam
Cranberry juice
Cream sour 10%
Creamer
Créme fraiche cheese
Cress
Crispbread
Crucian
Cucumber (bitter)

Cucumber (spicy cucumber)
Curcuma
Curd cheese 20%
Currant (black)
Currant (red)
Currant (white)
Currant jam (red)
Currants (black)
Currants (red)
Daisy
Dandelion (young plants)
Dandelion juice
Dandelionroots tea
Dashi
Dates dried
Dates red
Deer's Bones
Duck (slaughtered)
Ducks egg
Dulse (seaweed)
Dyer's broom herb
Eel
Elderberries
Elderberry blossom tee
Endive salad
Evening primrose oil
Fenugreek (Trigonella foenum-graecum)
Feta cheese
Feta cheese
Fig
Fish innards
Fish remains
Fish sauce
Flounder
Flower pollen
Fresh cheese
Fresh cheese from soya
Fresh cheese with herbs
Freshwater crab
Freshwater fish
Fructose (glucose)
Fruit tea
Gail plum
Galangal
Garam Masala powder
Gelatin white
Gelee Royal
Gentian root tea
Ginger oil
Ginkgo fruit
Ginseng
Ginseng root
Goat and sheep's milk

Goat cheese
Goose
Goose egg
Goose parts
Gooseberry
Grapefruit (Pomelo)
Grapefruit dried peel
Grapefruit juice
Grapes red
Grapes white
Grapeseed oil
Grass carp
Green spelt
Greengage
Ground
Guava
Halibut (Flatfish)
Hawthorn
Herbal tea mix
Herbs bitter
Herbs of Provence
Herbs various
Herbs wild
Herring
Hibiscus tea
Hijiki
Honey
Hop
Horehound leaves
Hyssop
Iceberg lettuce
Jasmine blossoms tee
Jellyfish
Juniper berry
Kaki plum
Kalmus
Kefir
King Solomon's-seal
Kiwi
Kombu seaweed (Saccharina japonica)
Kukicha tea
Kumquats
Ladyfingers
Lamb's lettuce
Lamb's lettuce
Lavender blossoms
Leaf salads (bitter)
Lemon
Lemon juice
Lemon peel
Lemongrass
Lentils black
Lentils red
Lentils yellow

Lettuce
Licorice root tea
Lime
Lime blossom tea
Linseed
Linseed (crushed)
Linseed oil
Liver smoothing tea
Longane
Loquate / Japanese medlar
Lotus roots
Lotus seeds
Lovage seeds
Luo Han Guo fruit
Lychee
Lychee in Preserved
Lye roll
Mackerel
Mallow (Malva sylvestris) blossom tea
Malt
Mango
Mare's milk
Marjoram
Mascarpone cheese
Medlar
Millet flakes
Mineral water
Mirabelle plum
Miso
Miso black (fermented)
Miso paste (soy bean paste)
Mixed Pickles
Mold cheese
Morel (black, dried)
Morel, dried
Mozzarella
Mu Erh Mushroom
Muesli
Mulberry fruit
Mulled Wine Spice
Mullet
Multi-grain bread (gray bread)
Mung bean sprouting
Mussels
Mustard
Mustard Dijon
Mustard medium hot
Mustard seeds
Mustard sweet
Nasturtium (nose-twister or nose-tweaker)
Nectarine
Noodles (wheat) with egg
Noodles (wheat, lasagne) with egg

Noodles (wheat, ribbon noodles) with egg
Noodles (wheat, spaghetti) with egg
Noodles (whole grain) with egg
Nori, purple seaweed, red algae
Oat
Oat flakes (whole grain)
Oat flakes roasted
Oat flour
Oat fusion (baby food)
Oat meal
Oat milk
Octopus
Octopus
Olive oil
Olives
Olives green
Orange
Orange blossom
Orange dried peel
Orange grated peel
Orange jam
Orange peel
Oyster mushroom
Oyster shell powder
Oysters
Palm oil
Papaya
Passion blossoms tea
Passion fruit
Peaches
Peaches (canned)
Peanut butter
Peanut oil
Pearl barley
Pearl barley
Peas
Pepper powder (hot)
Peppermint
Peppers (rose peppers)
Peppers (sweet)
Peppers powder
Perch
Pheasant
Pickle
Pigeon
Pigeon egg
Pimento
Pineapple
Pineapple juice without sugar
Pinto beans speckled
Plaice
Plum
Plum dried

Plums
Pomegranate
Poppy
Potato flour
Prickly pear
Processed cheese 12%
Psyllium seed
Pudding powder vanilla
Puff pastry
Pumpernickel (dark bread)
Pumpkin seed oil
Pumpkin seeds
Quince
Quinoa
Rabbit
Rabbit meat
Radicchio
Radish
Radish (white, green, purple-red)
Radish leaves
Raisins
Rapeseed oil
Raspberry
Raspberry dried (immature)
Raspberry jam
Raspberry leaf tea
Red beet
Red berry (without sugar)
Red cabbage
Reishi mushroom
Rhubarb
Ribworttea
Rice (fragrance)
Rice (Gaoliang / Sorghum)
Rice (whole grain)
Rice Basmati
Rice black
Rice flour
Rice long grain rice
Rice malt
Rice mash
Rice noodles
Rice red
Rice round grain
Rice starch
Rice sticky
Rice sweet
Rice variety any
Rice wild (nature rice)
Romaine lettuce / lettuce salad
Rose blossom tea
Rose hip
Rose leaf tea
Rosefish

Rosemary
Rucola
Rusk
Rye
Rye flour
Rye wholemeal bread
Safflower (Dyer's thistle / Hong Hua)
Saffron
Sage
Sago (cereals)
Sake
Salmon
Sea buckthorn
Sea cucumber
Seacrab
Sesame oil
Sesame oil roasted
Sesame, white
Shark
Sheep's milk
Sheep's milk yoghurt
Shiitake, dried
Shrimp
Shrimps
Skim milk powder
Slug
Sorrel
Sour cherries
Sour cream 15% fat
Sour milk
Sour milk cheese 20%
Sourdough
Soy flour
Soy noodles
Soy sauce
Soy Tofu smoked
Soybean milk
Soybean oil
Soybeans, black
Soybeans, blacks, fermented
Spelled (Dark) bread
Spelled flakes
Spelled grain
Spelled semolina
Spelled wholemeal flour
Spiny lobsters
Spurdog (spiny dogfish, Schillerlocken)
St. Benedict's thistle, blessed thistle,
holy thistle, spotted thistle
Star anise
Stevia (candyleaf, sweetleaf)
Strawberries
Strawberry jam
Strawberry Juice

Sugar fructose - fruit sugar
Sugar glucose - grapes sugar
Sugar Milk Sugar
Sugar substitute (sweetener)
Sunflower oil
Supplementary nutrition
Tangerine
Tarragon (Estragon)
Tea mixture uric acid lowering
Thistle oil
Thyme
Thyme dried
Toast bread (whole grain)
Tomato dried
Tonic Water
Trout
Trout (smoked)
Truffle
Tsampa (roasted barley flour)
Tuna
Turkey breast meat
Turkey ham
Turnip
Umeboshi paste
Umeboshi plums (Japanese apricots)
Valerian
Vanilla
Vanilla powder
Vanilla sugar natural
Vinegar (Apple vinegar)
Vinegar (Red wine vinegar)
Vinegar Aceto Balsamico
Vinegar Aceto Balsamico white
Wakame
Walnut oil
Water
Water hot
Watermelon
Wheat
Wheat bulgur
Wheat flakes
Wheat flour
Wheat germ oil
Wheat semolina
Wheat semolina for children
Wheatgrass juice
Wheatgrass powder
Whey
White beans
Whitefish
Wild garlic (garlic spinach)
Wild herbs
Wild strawberries
Wormwood

Wormwood herb
Yam root, yam root tuber
Yeast
Yew nut

Yoghurt vanilla
Yogi tea
Yogurt (natural, 1.5% fat)
Yogurt (natural, 3.5% fat)

10.3 Use ingredients: little

Beans (green, fresh)
Beef bone marrow
Beef fillet
Beef meat
Beef meat (calf)
Beef meatbones
Beef soup meat
Beef stomach
Beer (Pils)
Beer (Top-fermented German dark beer)
Bitter liqueur
Black beans
Black tea
Broad beans (thick beans)
Brown ale
Bush beans
Campari
Cauliflower
Chicken egg
Chicken egg white
Chicken yolk
Chickpeas
Chili (pod or ground)
Chocolate
Chocolate (Diabetic)
Clarified butter
Coconut fat
Coconut flakes
Coconut milk
Cola drink (low calorie)
Cream (30% fat)
Cream sour 20%
Cream sour 30%
Cream, sweet 30%
Curd cheese 40%
Curry
Curry paste red
Deer meat
Deer meat
Edam cheese
Eel smoked
Emmental cheese
Fernet Branca (herbal bitter liqueur)
Fig dried
French beans

Ginseng liqueur
Goat
Goat and sheep's brain
Goose fat
Gorgonzola
Gouda cheese
Honey wine (Met)
Horse meat
Kidney beans (red)
Lamb bones
Lamb meat
Lamb shoulder
Leek
Lentils
Lima beans
Lobster
Lychee liqueur
Margarine (diet)
Martini
Mayonnaise 50%
Mayonnaise 80%
Millet
Mung bean
Mutton
Onion (shallot)
Onion (spring onion)
Onion read
Onion white
Parmesan
Peanuts
Pepper (ground)
Pepper Cayenne
Pepper white (ground)
Peppercorns
Pepperoni
Pepperoni, red, pitted, halved
Pepperoni, yellow, pitted, halved
Pine nuts
Pineapple (from a can)
Pistachios
Pork Bacon
Pork brain
Pork ham
Pork ham cooked
Pork ham smoked
Pork knuckle

Pork Lard
Pork liver
Pork meat
Pork skin
Pork stomach
Pork's intestine
processed cheese 30%
Prosecco
Quail
Quail egg
Rabbit (wild)
Red wine
Salt
Salt (herbal)
Sauerkraut (cutted cabbage fermented)
Savoy cabbage / kale
Sesame paste (Tahini)
Sherry (whine)
Soy Tofu
Soya Cuisine (soy cream)
Soybeans
Soybeans, yellow
Sugar - icing sugar

Sugar brown
Sugar candy white
Sugar cane sugar
Sugar molasses
Sugar palm sugar
Sugar white
Sunflower seeds
Tabasco
Walnuts
Walnuts roasted
Wheat beer
Wheat flatbread/pita bread
White bread (baguette)
White bread (pretzel sticks)
White bread (roll)
White bread (wheat bread)
White breadcrumbs
White cabbage
White dumpling bread (wheat bread cut into chunks)
White wine
Wild boar meat

10.4 Do not use contra-acting foods

Almond milk
Almond puree
Beef heart
Beef heart (calf)
Beef kidney
Beef liver
Beef lungs (calf)
Beef Oxtail pieces
Brazil nuts
Chicken Blood
Chicken heart
Chicken liver
Chicken stomach
Cooking oil
Deer's kidneys
Duck (heart)
Goat and sheep's blood
Goat and sheep's liver

Goat and sheep's stomach
Goose blood
Hazelnuts
Lamb kidneys
Lamb liver
Margarine
Mutton
Peanut (roasted)
Pig blood
Pork fat (lard)
Pork heart
Pork kidneys
Pork lung
Pork marrow bones
Pork sausage (Bratwurst) Pork/beef sausage (smoked)
Rabbit liver
Rum
Spirit

11 Herbs and their effects

11.1 Basil

It has a beneficial effect on flatulence and nausea, relaxing and soothing.

Good to fight emphysema, bronchitis, whooping cough, high blood pressure, headache, mouth odor, warts, hiccup, gout, migraine.

11.2 Nettles

Promotes urination. Tea or juice, cleanses the blood and the kidneys, supports prostate problems, inhibit the formation of inflammation, pain-relieving.

11.3 Dill

The medicinal and spice herb has an antispasmodic effect and stimulates gastric juice production. Good to fight flatulence. Antispasmodic for gastrointestinal discomfort.

11.4 Coriander

The essential oils are appetizing, digestive, cramping and soothing in stomach and intestinal disorders.

11.5 Herbs various

Appetizing, lots of trace elements and vitamins

11.6 Cress

Diuretic, supports urination. Good to fight dry mouth, inner agitation, sore throat, diabetes, kidney stones, gastrointestinal complaints, lung problems, menstrual cramps or cancer.

11.7 Chives

Bactericide, prevents cancer, strengthens gastric juice production, promotes digestion and blood circulation, promotes growth, triggers stagnation.

11.8 Lovage

Stimulates digestion, reduces pain. Extracts of the root are used to flush out urinary tract infections and prevent kidney gravel.

11.9 Dandelion (young plants)

Detoxifies, relieves inflammation. Regulates digestion, helps with rheumatism, releases kidney stones, leaves pimples and chronic skin disorders disappear.

11.10 Oregano fresh

It has an anti-digestive, calming and nerve-strengthening effect, helps to fight cramping stomach and intestinal disorders. The ingredient Carvacrol has an anti-inflammatory effect.

11.11 Oregano dried

It has an anti-digestive, calming and nerve-strengthening effect, helps to fight cramping stomach and intestinal disorders. The ingredient Carvacrol has an anti-inflammatory effect.

11.12 Parsley

Stimulates liver function, detoxifies. Forces urinating. Relieves flatulence. Digestive and menstrual stimulating, birth-accelerating, memory-enhancing, blood-purifying, skin-smoothing.

11.13 Peppermint

Relaxes, frees the lungs and the nose (inhale), regulates the cycle. Stimulates bile flow and bile production, antispasmodic in gastrointestinal disorders, antimicrobial and antiviral.

11.14 Rosemary

Promotes digestion, relieves bloating, strengthens lung, spleen and kidney. Affects the circulation and nerves. Appetizing. Baths help to fight circulatory disorders as well as with gout and rheumatism.

11.15 Sage

Good to fight yeast infections. The leaves have a digestive effect and are used in greasy foods. Antiperspirant effect. Helps to relieve coughing attacks. Dries out (TCM).

11.16 Blackthorn (Sloe)

The blossoms, bark and fruits are astringent, diuretic, weakly laxative, fever-shedding, stomach-enhancing and anti-inflammatory.

11.17 Black caraway

Detoxifying, immunoregulatory. In addition, the oil should stimulate the formation of bone marrow cells and generally protect body cells from viruses.

11.18 Thyme dried

Disinfecting. It stimulates the blood circulation, increases the appetite and helps to digest fat meat better. Strengthens lungs and spleen (TCM).

11.19 Lemongrass

Reduction of flatulence, antimicrobial, appetizing. Prevention of influenza. Good to fight infections in the mouth and throat.

11.20 Lemon Balm

Stimulating, antibacterial, encouraging, relaxing, antispasmodic, cooling, antipyretic, analgesic, sweat-inducing, virus-inhibiting. Good for colds, fever, flu, cough, bronchitis, asthma, loss of appetite, bloating, heartburn.

12 Basics of Nutrition

The basic principles of nutrition described herein are general recommendations. They are not aimed at a specific form of therapy. Recommendations concerning a therapy have priority.

12.1 Nutrition

Regular meals in a relaxed atmosphere. A warm breakfast is considered a good start into the day.
The main meals ought to be taken for lunch – supper in the early evening. Pay attention to feeling hungry or sated: don't eat too much nor remain hungry is the rule
Prepare the meals freshly from natural, regional products. Frozen, heat-conserved, industrially prepared or foodstuffs cooked in the microwave oven are rejected.
Choice of foodstuffs according to the season: more cooling food in summer, more warming food in winter.
Eat cooked food at least twice a day. Food and drinks ought to be lukewarm, never ice-cold or hot.
Raw vegetables, briefly cooked vegetables, freshly squeezed juices and mineral water are not recommended. Milk and dairy products are only included in the diet if they don't cause problems.
Don't use therapeutic recipes over a longer period without consulting your doctor or therapist.

Varied food
Enjoy the diversity of foodstuffs. Characteristics of a balanced nutrition are variety, suitable combination and a balanced quantity of rich and low energy foodstuffs (on one hand avoiding undersupply with essential nutrients and on the other hand to take to many undesirable substances).

A lot of Cereal Products - and Potatoes
Bread, pasta, rice, cereal flakes (best wholemeal) as well as potatoes contain almost no fat, but many vitamins, mineral nutrients, trace elements, roughage and secondary plant substances. These foodstuffs ought to be taken with low-fat side dishes.

Vegetables and Fruit – „Take Five" every day ...
5 portions of vegetables and fruit a day, as fresh as possible, briefly cooked, or maybe one portion as a juice – ideal as a side dish to every meal as well as snack between meals: Thus a lot of vitamins, mineral nutrients as well as roughage and secondary plant substances

Daily milk and dairy products
Milk and Dairy Products every Day, once or twice per Week Fish; meat, sausages as well as eggs moderately. These foodstuffs contain valuable nutrients like calcium in the milk, iodine selenium and omega-3 fat acids in saltwater fish. Meat is favorable due to its high content of disposable iron and the vitamins B1, B6 and B12. Quantities of 300 – 600 g meat and sausage per week are sufficient. Prefer low-fat products, especially in meat- and dairy products.

Low-fat and fatty Foodstuffs
Fat supplies us with essential fat acids and fatty foodstuffs contain also fat-soluble vitamins. Fat is high in energy; therefore much fat in the food may cause overweight, possibly also cancer. Too many saturated fat acids may further a tendency for cardio-vascular diseases in the long term. Prefer vegetable oils and fats (e.g. rapeseed-, olive-, soya-oils and solid fats produced therefrom). Beware of invisible fat in meat- and dairy products, pastry and sweets as well as in fast-food and convenience foods. 70 – 90 g fat per day is sufficient.

Moderately Sugar and Salt
Take sugar and foods/drinks containing various kinds of sugar (e.g. glucose syrup) only occasionally. Use herbs and spices as well as a little salt creatively. Prefer salt containing iodine.

Plenty of Liquids
Water is absolutely essential. Drink 1-2 l liquids every day. Prefer water (with or without gas) and other low-calorie drinks. Alcoholic drinks should not be taken.

Tasty Dishes, carefully cooked
Cook the meals with as low temperatures and as short as possible, using little water and fat – this preserves the original taste, keeps the nutrients intact and prevents the production of harmful compounds.

Take time and enjoy the food
Take your Time and enjoy your Food
Eating consciously helps to eat right. The eye enjoys food, too. It's fun, invites to enjoy varied dishes and stimulates the feeling of satiety.

Watch your Weight and stay in Motion
A balanced diet and a lot of exercise and sport (30 – 60 min/day) are a healthy combination. The right weight furthers well-being and health. Thermals, directional effectiveness, digestive power

There are various criteria for judging the effectiveness of herbs and foodstuffs.

The use of certain herbs and ingredients is based on observations of the effects on the body which these foodstuffs, herbs and spices show after having eaten them. The medical science has developed following system: Every ingredient or herb has a directional effectiveness. Furthermore, there are herbs which have a special effect on certain organs.

The basic condition for a healthy metabolism is to obtain sufficient energy from food and that the digestive process doesn't use too much energy. An easily digestible meal makes content and sated, doesn't cause flatulence and fatigue after the meal. The perfect spices increase the healthiness of our meals. Very often, just small doses of herbs and spices will suffice. They are not used to make us sated, but to help our digestive organs to digest the food.

12.2 Recipes

The recipes list the ingredients to be used and the cooking instructions show how the dish is prepared. The list of ingredients shows the concerned quantities as well as the relevance for the therapy. If you find „less than mentioned", try to comply or find an alternative from the „list of recommended foodstuffs". Mostly it shall result just in a small change of taste when you simply avoid this ingredient.

Mild cooking methods: boiling, stewing, poaching, steaming
Strong cooking methods: barbecuing, roasting, frying, smoking
Balanced cooking methods: deep-frying, baking brick
Deep-freezing and warming in the microwave oven should be avoided (denaturalization).

12.3 Foodstuffs

Foodstuffs have an effect on body and soul like medicinal herbs, only a very much milder one. Dietary advice is mainly based on regional foodstuffs. The knowledge about the effects of each foodstuff and the knowledge, when which foodstuff shall be used, is based on the orthodoschool of medicine. Use ecologic-organic products, if possible. As everything should be cooked for a long time due to a better digestability and very rarely eaten raw, the food agrees with everyone.

The classification of the foodstuffs according to their effect on the body is the basis in order to achieve a harmonious status of health.

Dietary advisors do not recommend certain foodstuffs for everyone. The individual diet is tailor-made for the individual constitution.

Buy only fresh and ripe fruit and vegetables. You ought to leave unripe fruit and vegetables and such with brown spots and wilted leaves behind in the market. In this case take deep-frozen goods (never ready-to-serve dishes!). Fruit and vegetables are deep-frozen immediately after harvesting and often contain more vitamins and minerals than the goods from the vegetable shelf. Whereas conserved or tinned goods contain very much less biological substances. Also, salt, sugar and others are mostly added to the latter. Never leave the foodstuffs in the water after washing them to avoid that many vital substances get drowned. Clean salads, fruit and vegetables immediately before serving.

Please make sure of the hygienic processing of foodstuffs. Clean your salads, fruit and vegetables carefully. When cooking with meat, prepare all ingredients first and then process the meat products. Clean the worktop and tools very carefully. Wooden surfaces ought to be treated with a mild disinfectant regularly in order to reduce germination.

Store fruit and vegetables separately, if possible. Harvested fruit and vegetables are still alive and emit e.g. ethylene gas, which makes other products ripen and age faster. Keep meat and fish in the closed packaging or store them in the fridge in closed containers.

12.4 Herbs

There are some basic rules for storing medicinal herbs. On principle, herbs must be protected from direct sunlight, humidity and heat.

Containers for the storage of herbs may be glasses, ceramic jars and even plastic containers. However, plastic is a rather unsuitable material and should only be a short-term solution. In case of glass containers, use a dark material.

Medicinal herbs cannot be kept for any long period. The shelf life of herbs is limited. However, it can be prolonged with suitable storage. The place should be dark, rather cool and absolutely dry. A wooden medicine cabinet, placed not directly next to a source of heat, would be ideal. Never buy large quantities of herbs so as not to have to throw them away. Label the container with the name of the herb and the date of harvesting or processing.

13 Other dietic-books

The following syndromes of dietetics, TCM or for a therapy supplement for cancer are available.

Dietetics

E001. Nutrition of the infant - baby food
E002. Nutrition during lactation
E003. Nutrition in old age
E004. Nutrition of children and adolescents
E005. Nutrition of athletes
E006. Light weight
E007. Pregnancy
E008. Full food

Protein and electrolyte - kidneys
E009. (hemodialysis) dialysis treatment
E010. Acute renal failure
E011. Chronic renal insufficiency
E012. Nephrotic syndrome
E013. Kidney stones (nephrolithiasis)

Gastrointestinal tract - pancreas
E014. Acute pancreatitis (inflammation of the pancreas)
E015. Chronic pancreatitis (inflammation of the pancreas)

Gastrointestinal tract - small intestine and large intestine
E016. Acute obstipation (constipation)
E017. Chronic obstipation (constipation)
E018. Colon irritabile
E019. Diverticulitis
E020. Acquired lactose intolerance (lactose malabsorption)
E021. Fructose malabsorption
E022. Glutensensitive enteropathy (celiac disease)
E023. Colectomy
E024. Short Bowel Syndrome

Gastrointestinal tract - liver, gallbladder, bile ducts
E025. Acute and chronic hepatitis (inflammation of the liver)
E026. Cholelithiasis (bile stones)
E027. fatty liver
E028. cirrhosis

Gastrointestinal tract - Stomach and duodenal intestine
E029. Acute gastritis
E030. Chronic gastritis
E031. Stomach bleeding
E032. Ulcus ventriculi and duodenal ulcer
E033. Condition after gastric surgery

Gastrointestinal tract - oral cavity and esophagus
E034. Stomatitis
E035. Esophageal carcinoma (esophageal cancer)
E036. Refluosophagitis (heartburn)

Special diseases
E037. Phenylketonuria (PKU)
E038. Rheumatic joint diseases

Metabolism
E039. Obesity (overweight)
E040. Diabetes mellitus
E041. Eating disorders (underweight)

Fat metabolism
E042. Hypercholesterolaemia (increased cholesterol level)
E043. Hepatic Encephalopathy

Heart and circulation
E044. Arteriosclerosis (arterial calcification)
E045. Heart insufficiency
E046. Hypertension
E047. Hyperuricaemia and gout

Changed nutrient requirements
E048. In case of fever
E049. For malignant diseases
E050. After burns
E051. Radiation and chemotherapy

CANCER
E100. Pancreatic cancer
E101. Bladder cancer
E102. Blood cancer (leukemia)
E103. Breast cancer
E104. Colorectal cancer
E105. Gastric cancer
E106. Kidney cancer
E107. Esophageal cancer

TCM
E200. Bladder - moisture heat in the bladder
E201. Bladder - moisture and cold in the bladder
E202. Bladder - emptiness and cold in the bladder
E203. Large intestine - external cold affects the large intestine
E204. Large intestine - moisture heat in the large intestine
E205. Large intestine - heat blocks the intestine II acute
E206. Large intestine - dryness of the colon
E207. Large intestine - Yang deficiency (cold)
E208. Heart - Blood insufficiency
E209. Heart - Blood stagnation
E210. Heart - Fire
E211. Heart - Hot mucus clogs the heart pores

E212. Heart - Cold mucus clogs the heart pores
E213. Heart - Qi deficiency
E214. Heart - Yang deficiency
E215. Heart - Yin deficiency
E216. Liver - Ascending Liver Yang
E217. Liver - Blood deficiency
E218. Liver - Blood stagnation
E219. Liver - Moisture heat in liver and gall bladder
E220. Liver - Fire
E221. Liver - Gall bladder Qi-Empty
E222. Liver - Cold in the liver meridian
E223. Liver - Qi stagnation
E224. Liver - Wind
E225. Liver - Wind with ascending liver Yang
E226. Liver - Wind with blood anemic
E227. Liver - Wind with extreme heat
E228. Lung - Qi deficiency
E229. Lung - Mucus-moisture in the lungs
E230. Lung - Mucus-heat in the lungs
E231. Lung - Mucus-cold in the lungs
E232. Lung - Dryness of the lungs
E233. Lung - Wind-heat attacks the lungs
E234. Lung - Wind-cold affects the lungs
E235. Lung - Yin deficiency
E236. Stomach - Bloodstagnation
E237. Stomach - Fire
E238. Stomach - Cold with liquid
E239. Stomach - Nutrition stagnation
E240. Stomach - Qi deficiency
E241. Stomach - Rebellious Qi
E242. Stomach - Yin Emptiness
E243. Spleen - Heat and moisture attack the spleen
E244. Spleen - Coldness and moisture affects the spleen
E245. Spleen - Qi deficiency
E246. Spleen - Qi deficiency + Declining spleen Qi
E247. Spleen - Qi deficiency + spleen does not control the blood
E248. Spleen - Yang deficiency
E249. Kidney - Heart and kidney no longer communicate
E250. Kidney - Jing deficiency
E251. Kidney - Kidneys cannot receive the Qi
E252. Kidney - Qi is not stable
E253. Kidney - Yang deficiency
E254. Kidney - Yin deficiency

For further information visit di-book.com.